The Cautionary Heart 2: Blame

Synopsis

A mother's responsibility is to love her child unconditionally, even when controlling forces are out of her power. The diagnosis of mental illness can be devastating for any family, but Raven Harris embraced her son, Eric, and set up a plan for his life's journey. She convinced him to take his medication daily and work toward being a better version of himself. Raven ensured Eric was well-educated and able to climb the ladder of success. Even when he stumbled and failed, along the way, she was there to pick up the pieces and to motivate him never to give up.

Finally, Eric could leave the nest and take charge of his destiny. Even though he was out of her sight, Raven constantly reminded him to stay on the plans that he had followed throughout his life. Sometimes, life will throw you many curveballs. The way you handle it is up to you.

Do you accept accountability for your decisions? Or do you place the blame elsewhere?

Acknowledgments

I would like to thank God for giving me the courage to step outside of the box and continue putting the vision of this story and its contents to pen and paper. I would also like to thank my friend, Delphia Garland who continues to inspire and encourage me to keep going in my dream journey of writing. And lastly, to all of those who continue to support me in my venture.

Chapter 1

This is a day of sadness, not only for the family but more so for the mother, Raven, for the loss of her son, Thomas Eric Harris. His casket is pure gold, adorned with lavish fresh-cut flowers, and has his name laser engraved on the front. As the pallbearers approached the hearse, they slowly removed the casket and carefully carried it into the doors of Mountain Baptist Church behind Pastor Matthew Winters.

Barely able to stand from grief, Raven is behind the casket, wearing a black dress with a black velvet hat covered with a netted veil that extends over her eyes. Around her neck is a sterling silver chain with the cursive letter *R* encrusted in pure diamonds. Eric purchased it as a special gift for her weeks before his death. While they stood in the hallway, they could see the sun shining through the stained-glass windows and hear the somber music radiating throughout the church.

Walking arm in arm, Raven and her brother, Harold, were seated on the front row by the church ushers. While the rest of the family and friends were being seated, the pastor leaned in and softly whispered assurances into Raven's ear. She sits stone-faced, staring at the casket ahead of her; not one tear is rolling from her eyes, just a *stare*, appearing to be lost in her own little world. *Days before, Harold had her doctor come by the house, and Raven was given a sedative to help her sleep and rest comfortably.*

Pastor Matthew Winters enters the pulpit, and the services begin. After the last song, everyone quietly listened as friends and former coworkers shared their memories of Eric. It was no surprise that the only coworker to pay respects to Eric from USC was Andrew, who introduced him to Core's, the gym owned by Danielle Moore. After Eric's convoluted past was revealed in the media, USC distanced itself and refused interviews regarding his tenure with their university.

When the remembrance was over, without warning, Raven stood and walked toward the *open* casket as her brother looked on. She leaned down, secretly whispered into Eric's ear, kissed him on the cheek, turned, and walked slowly back to her seat. Even though Raven wasn't crying, Harold reached into his pocket and gave her his handkerchief. She took the handkerchief and rolled it in her hand like a stress ball as the pallbearers walked toward Eric's casket.

As the service came to an end, the casket was closed, and the pastors walked down from the pulpit and shook the hands of every family member. The organist began playing soft music as the pallbearers rolled the casket out of the church, with the pastor following close behind. Harold, with assistance from the ushers, takes hold of Raven's arms, holding her tightly, lifts her up, and walks out of the church to the waiting family limousine.

On the way to the gravesite, Harold and his daughter, Kathy Crane, attempted to engage in conversation with Raven, but she sat there calm, looking straight ahead with only her eyes blinking sporadically. Once they arrived, Pastor Winters said a prayer and ended it with the *Book of Common Prayer:* "We, therefore, commit this body to the ground, earth to earth, ashes to ashes, dust to dust," as the casket is lowered into the ground.

In an instant, loud screams from Raven are heard, and tears are running down her face. Nurses rush to assist Harold in calming her down. The shock of losing Eric was finally emerging and showed in a way that frightened Harold. After a few minutes, she settled down, and the nurses assisted her into the car. Raven had already lost her husband, and now her only son was gone too.

In his attempts to ease her pain, Harold promised to stay with her as long as she needed him. As the weeks went by, he found that Raven's pain had deepened into depression. He suggests she seek grief counseling and agrees to be there with her every step of the way. After several tries at trying to convince her to get help, she yells out at him to *"let her be"* and that she will be just fine. Her grieving has been overwhelming and close to unbearable, with sadness, moodiness, and restlessness.

While Raven pretends to appreciate Harold's concerns, she assures him that everything is okay. Right now, she is way too busy handling the remainder of Eric's estate. Raven explains to him that this is the only thing keeping her sane and sound. Seriously, at this point, she just really wants to be left alone. Apologetically, Harold packed his clothing and toiletries. He is making every effort to be more considerate and courteous by allowing her the time and space to grieve on her own. Harold assures her that he will always be praying for her and that she should call him if she needs anything, day or night. With a kiss on her forehead, he ended the conversation. She nods, and he leaves for home.

Raven's time to stop grieving will be a slow process, and it will be in her own time and in her own way. Making trips back and forth to Chicago to settle Eric's estate has, in some strange way, helped her feel closer to him.

Chapter 2

It has been almost two years since Thomas Eric Harris killed himself in the bathroom of the Chicago Amtrak station. Raven, his mother, is unable to get the images out of her head or the reason behind Eric's suicide. Dark thoughts have rattled around in her mind ever since it happened. Raven is adamant that *something or someone* caused her son to spiral out of control. She doesn't believe that the cause of Eric's suicide was his own volition, but triggers of a higher magnitude, and not in the way described by the Chicago police and the media. The information received from these sources is always condescending and dismissive.

To this day, the reminders of Eric's downfall are viewed negatively at the counters of grocery stores and big box stores. On the front pages of every tabloid, like The Enquirer, the Star, and the Sun, are the worst pictures of Eric that they could find. Most of my close friends and family members say the pictures were photoshopped to make him look like an evil monster. Everybody seems to be against him, regardless of his mental disability. Whatever the case may be, Raven is now on a mission to seek more honest and truthful information about what happened to her son. In the last year, numerous television outlets have approached her often regarding movie deals that she has refused on many occasions. *She had no intention of exploiting her son for personal gain.*

As Raven was surfing the TV channels, she came across a documentary about her son and his victims. She watched as John Schmidt of 20/20 introduced the story. She heard, finally, for the first time, never-before-seen interviews from those who encountered Eric's wrath. Raven calmly sits to watch, leaning forward with her fingers intertwined across her waist. She attentively listens to Kimberly Casey, Danielle Moore, numerous USC employees, and others for their accounts of how her son affected their lives. Raven could not help wondering how each of them knew Eric and how well.

Although the picture painted of him is damning, she does accept the fact that Eric did suffer from a mental illness that is clearly documented. But still, questions remain. Raven wanted answers to the potential cause or causes of what could have led Eric to the breaking point for him to commit such heinous crimes. As she listened closely to Kimberly Casey, Raven needed more in-depth knowledge of her son's involvement or relationship with her. Wiping tears from her eyes, she just could not shake the feeling that her son would have done all these bad things described.

Leaning back on the sofa, Raven became angrier and angrier as she watched the documentary, specifically the interviews of both Kim and Danielle, the two women who endured the most pain and suffering from Eric. The more she listened to them, the more she made it her mission to find out more about the two of them and how they came to know her son. It was no secret that Eric had philandering ways, and there was nothing described in any of the reports she'd heard that would give her pause regarding his indiscretions.

As she reminisced about his life, Raven became more obsessed with finding out what caused her son to descend into a world of darkness. The interviews describing her son made no sense to her. Former news reports did not offer much about any of the individuals interviewed. Now that is an angle to pursue, she deemed. During the commercial break, she "*googled*" and obtained whatever information she could find about the so-called victims.

As she heard the 20/20 intro, Raven raised her head and continued listening to Kimberly Casey, the soft-spoken woman, as she said, "I am not a victim; I'm a survivor." Raven started to feel Kimberly Casey had more involvement with Eric than Danielle Moore. So, the question remained regarding Danielle: how did she fit into the triangle?

Raven was due to return to Chicago in a few days to complete the settlement of Eric's estate and any other business he had. She could not believe all the business dealings he was involved in and the slow process it took to handle each of them. The good thing was that they were all legitimate, and she had no problems securing what was his. She hoped this would be the last trip she would ever have to make in the Windy City and that everything would be over and done with as far as his affairs were concerned.

There were still the off-shore business expenses she had to endure soon. The money recovered from city banks, Eric's home safe, and the briefcase full of money found on him at the time of his death were a total surprise to her, and there wasn't much paperwork involved. On the other hand, the off-shore closures would need more time and paperwork than she had anticipated, and now she was on her way to completing them.

Because of the documentary, Raven was now equipped with the names of individuals and the faces of those involved with her son during his time in Chicago. This would be her final mission for being there, and hopefully to give her closure. Would any of them be willing to talk to her about her son? After all, she was his mother, she thought.

In Raven's mind, she felt she had the right to know anything that could shed light on his demeanor or if there was anything that would help her understand. In particular, who or what would push him to end his own life instead of turning himself into the police? Obviously, she was looking for someone else to blame for Eric's violent tenancy and demise.

Sitting on the side of the bed, Raven thought about what Harold had said about a grief counselor. He didn't understand that I needed answers to the many questions on my mind before I could properly grieve, as I did for my husband. Subsequently, Raven decided to give all her thoughts some rest until she reached Chicago. As she placed her head on the pillow and closed her eyes, the words of Kimberly Casey echoed in her mind. She bizarrely repeated: "He is a victim, and he didn't survive."

Chapter 3

After all the plane flights back and forth over the past year, Raven decided she would drive to Chicago for this final trip and stay at the Wilshire Hotel. She was scheduled to meet with the CEO of the off-shore establishments that Eric had business dealings with the following day. The drive from Detroit, Michigan, had her tired, so to be well-rested, she took a shower, dressed in something comfortable, and ordered room service for dinner.

Sitting on the sofa in her suite, Raven picked up the newspaper from the coffee table to pass the time until her dinner arrived. Lo and behold, there was a story regarding the upcoming wedding of Kimberly Casey to Xander Carlisle. As she reads further, there is a picture of the two of them. Now that's interesting, she thought to herself. Ms. Casey appears to have a fascinating life among Chicago elites. The story mentions how much Kim previously suffered at the hands of Thomas Eric Harris and how she had risen from the ordeal and moved on with her life. Hundreds of congratulatory comments and well wishes are posted following the story. "Huh, so she's that popular in this city, and she's marrying out of her race," Raven whispered to herself.

After reading enough of the story of Kim and Xander, Raven unpacked, placing clothing in the closet and dresser drawers. Grabbing her laptop off the top of the dresser, she decided to Google the address and location of Kim's interior design business and Danielle's gym. To her surprise, both businesses are near one another.

Raven closed up her laptop and got her mind back on more pressing business. She had to make one last trip to Eric's former home before the Realty Company took possession. Raven also wanted to take more time to look for the key to the safe she found when she packed his things over a year ago. During their search, the police discovered large sums of money in the house, but months after the inquiry, they concluded there was no illegal connection. Since she is the sole beneficiary of his estate, Raven was given it all. She had cleared the home of furniture, selling it all, including expensive paintings, sculptures, and other valuable items. Eric concealed much more than she thought. Raven knew he was doing well from what he had described regarding his position at USC, but there was nothing she found that would have justified all the money she was now in possession of, with more to come. Besides dealing with the off-shore issues, she had one last bank to go to, where the paperwork had already been completed.

There was a knock at the door, followed by a man announcing room service. Raven's dinner had arrived. She figured that with all of the money she had inherited from Eric's estate and her finances, she could not only live well but eat well too. As she was eating, she checked her itinerary for the following day. Apart from the business dealings, she also wanted to do some sightseeing, shopping, and maybe take in a Broadway show before leaving. Raven yawned, finding the dinner and wine fulfilling, and began to feel a little drowsy. She took a warm shower and went to bed for a good night's sleep.

Raven awoke the next morning to the phone ringing on the nightstand. She had scheduled an automated wake-up call and was slow to get out of bed due to the overkill of wine consumption the night before. Finally, she allowed her feet to hit the floor and got up to dress. After moving around the room, Raven enjoyed breakfast with coffee and dressed. She was now wide awake and ready for the day ahead.

Raven's first stop is at Eric's home. She would need to contact the Realty Company afterward and then go to Central City Bank.

As she entered Eric's house, her footsteps seemed to be louder as she scurried across the empty floors. She looked everywhere around the house but had no luck finding the safe key, or any key for that matter. If the officers had found a key, Raven believed the police department would have contacted her. There was no combination lock on the safe; otherwise, she would have sought other measures to get it open. Raven finally gave up, locked up the house, called the Realty Company, letting them know she had completed the walk-through, and then left for the bank.

When Raven arrived at the bank, she was given a key and then taken by a bank official to Eric's safe deposit box. The official opened the vault, handed her the deposit box, and then left her in privacy. Raven opened the box with the key and was astonished at the contents. A small velvet drawstring bag was there. It contained a "key." Right away, she thought it was the key to the mystery safe found in Eric's home. There were also stocks, bonds, more cash wrapped in a rubber band, and a small burgundy box. When she opened it, there was a 1.7-carat princess-cut diamond engagement ring. Underneath the velvet cushioning, there was the receipt. Raven unraveled it and gasped. The receipt showed the cost of the ring was $15,000. She wondered who the ring was for. Was it for Kimberly, Danielle, or someone else? Raven had to find out who the intended woman was, one way or another. Raven gathered up everything in the box, placed it in her tote bag, and waited patiently to sign the paperwork to close the account. The more she investigated Eric's Chicago life, the more mystifying and intriguing it became. In the back of her mind, Raven wondered how Marcus Blackstone, one of Eric's friends from his childhood, was involved. There was a brief mention of him in the documentary, but nothing of significant value.

The bank officer left his office and informed Raven that he would be with her shortly. She picked up a magazine featuring a young boy, which evoked memories of Marcus's childhood. She recalled him as a bully and a troublemaker in his youth. Raven warned Eric on many occasions that he was not a good person to be around and urged him to choose his friends wisely. It appears he went against her advice. Maybe, she thought, Marcus might be able to give her some insight into Eric's life in Chicago. With that in mind, Raven decided she would also make a little visit to the jail while she was in Chicago. "This trip will take a lot longer than I originally expected," she said out loud. Maybe she would be able to get answers to some of her questions.

Chapter 4

It is days from the grand wedding of Kimberly Casey and Xander Carlisle. The previous year, they both sold their residences and built a bigger home in the suburbs, all the while making plans for the wedding and continuing to work. It was a lot, given their hectic schedules, but they were enjoying it all. There had been bridal showers, parties, luncheons, and dinners, and they were now burned out from all the hoopla. Kim was looking dead on her feet and sluggish while sitting in her office.

Xander walked by, noticing how exhausted she appeared. He stopped in. "Are you okay?" he asked. "Yeah, I just need to catch my breath," Kim replied. Everything has been non-stop in the last few months, and I probably just need to rest from it all. "Is there anything I can do to help?" he asked. No, Danielle is taking care of everything, so I think we're okay for now. She's been my saving grace in all of this. Okay, but don't hesitate to ask because I realize how stressed you've been with the wedding and work. Maybe you should take some time off and not accept any further projects, at least until after the wedding. Monica and I can handle the day-to-day responsibilities. I'll even take half-days off so that we can spend some time together, he suggested. "That does sound good, but do you think it'll be okay?" Kim asked. I only have one project left to complete, and meetings are scheduled for two more. I can probably reschedule them because the clients don't seem to be in that much of a hurry. My schedule should be clear after that. Sure, everything will be okay, Xander assured her.

We can discuss it with Monica, and then go from there. Good idea! I wouldn't want her to feel that we're abandoning her, Kim said, looking concerned. I'm sure she won't, sweetheart. Monica adores you and has mentioned to me at times that you looked like you needed some rest, so I have no doubt she will be more than happy to pitch in, except for the design portion, of course, he said, smiling. That put a smile on Kim's face. "Monica has already left for the day. We can get together with her in the morning.

In the meantime, I am going to finish up here, and you, my darling, get your things together because we're going out for a quiet dinner, if you're feeling up to it," Xander suggested. Despite her discomfort, she managed to put on a brave face so as not to ruin his dinner plans. Sounds good; I'll meet you at the elevator, Kim replied.

Kim rose from her desk and had to catch herself, nearly falling back in her chair from dizziness. She stood there for a moment, holding onto the desk, then walked over to her small office fridge. Feeling queasy and light-headed, Kim grabbed a small bottle of water, believing she may just have a severe case of dehydration. After gulping down half of the bottle, she started to feel a little better. Slowly and gently, she gathers her things and meets up with Xander at the elevator.

After dining at McCormick and Schmidt's, the drive home was upsetting Kim's stomach, and she started to feel nauseous. About a mile from home, she screamed for Xander to stop the car. He slammed on the brake. "What is it?" Kim opened the door and started regurgitating repeatedly. Xander immediately put the car in park, jumped out, and ran to the passenger side to help Kim out of the car. He looked at her, saw panic on her face, and said he was taking her to the hospital right now. Xander grabbed a few tissues from the box in the backseat for her.

Slowly, Kim's vomiting ceased. Xander helped her back into the car, and he rushed to the emergency room of Memorial Hospital. He parked near the automatic doors and helped Kim out of the car. He was panicking while telling personnel at the desk that something was wrong with his fiancé. Xander was assisted quickly, as one nurse rushed from behind the desk with an emesis basin and took hold of Kim, and another one grabbed a wheelchair and wheeled her back to an examination room while directing Xander to the waiting area.

Nervously, Xander sat nervously waiting for the doctor to return with his report of Kim's health issues. It seemed like hours before the doctor came out with Kim. Xander jumped up when he saw them. Kim looked better than she did when he initially brought her in, about an hour or so ago. Xander turned to the doctor and asked if she was okay. Ms. Casey will be fine, as he handed her a prescription for nausea and vomiting. "I'll let the two of you talk, and Ms. Casey, take care of yourself and remember to follow-up with your physician," the doctor replied. Kim swore the doctor to confidentiality about her illness. I will, and thank you, doctor. Okay, what's going on? Xander questioned. We'll talk when we get home. But everything's okay, right? as he looked at her with concern. Yes, everything is fine, just fine, Kim replied, setting his mind at ease.

On the way home, Xander made small talk until he pulled into the garage. Kim, feeling weak, was assisted out of the car and into the house. "Would you like something to drink?" he asked as he helped her to the sofa. Sure, how about you open up a bottle of wine so you can take the edge off and bring me a bottle of sparkling water with a wedge of lemon? Are you sure? he asked. "Yes, and stop looking so worried," she smiled. Okay, coming right up! he said, attempting to initiate happy vibes.

Xander carefully poured himself a glass of wine, while Kim took sips of the sparkling water. Now, tell me, what did the doctor say? Why were you so sick after dinner? Were you allergic to something that you ate? Was it food poisoning? because if so, we need to get... Slow down, my love. None of those reasons. It is because... "WE'RE PREGNANT!" she shouted.

It took Xander a moment; he was in shock, then realized what Kim had just sprung on him. He jumped up and pulled her up from the sofa, kissing and hugging her tightly. He thought about what he was doing and stopped, pulled away, and looked at her. "Sorry, I don't want to mash the baby," Xander jokily said. "Is the doctor sure? Are you sure we are pregnant?" he asked. Yes, we are. In fact, she said, we are nearly two months in. Awesome! as he exhaled. Oh man, this is great news! Okay, what is it that I need to do now? he asked breathlessly. There is nothing you need to do but love me as you always have. I think that I can do that while simultaneously saluting her.

Wow! Our parents are going to be ecstatic! I know, so that's why I am asking that we wait and tell them after the wedding, Kim suggested. I don't want to put too much on their plate before then. And Danielle, we need to keep it from her too, because she cannot hold water, and they laughed hard. Good idea, Xander agreed through his laughter. It won't be that long. The wedding is in four days, then we can make arrangements to take our parents to dinner and tell them before they fly home. That would be great, Kim replied. In the meantime, I will handle telling Danielle.

Xander looked at Kim lovingly and asked, "Are you happy, sweetheart?" I'm thrilled, she said, beaming at him. And you, how are you feeling about all of this? Can't you see that I cannot let go of the smile on my face? Xander responded with excitement!

"We need to start putting together a nursery," Kim announced. Oh no, you don't, not you. I will handle that, but you can supervise and decide on the décor, he said. I do not want to see you pick up anything heavier than a pencil. Yes, sir! I mean it, Kim. You have worked enough over the last few months, and now you need rest, and those my lady, are Dr. Carlisle's orders. I do not want you dropping at the altar, he said, smiling at her. I will, really, I will, she said. And we might want to consider getting you a housekeeper while we wait on our bundle of joy. I think that is a good idea.

Meanwhile, I need to make sure that my dress will not need any additional alterations because it did feel a little snug when I had my last fitting. Okay, take Monica with you, because Danielle may start asking questions. We don't need anything that will promote stress or let the cat out of the bag. No problem; she has been nothing short of a good friend since we talked things out. Sometimes, I think she goes a little overboard. I believe she continues to feel responsible for what happened to us two years ago. Time and time again, I have tried to ease her mind that we are over it and moving on, the both of us.

Hopefully, the wedding will cheer her up, he commented. I'm sure she will be fine, Kim chimed in. She appears now to be more occupied with the lavish dress I chose for her to wear. And now that everything has been taken care of, she has finally begun to relax and show off her sunny personality. Honestly, I think Danielle found a lot of joy in helping with the wedding. She takes her position as matron of honor seriously and has been by my side every step of the way. That will keep her busy for a while, he laughed.

Oh, remember, we need to talk with Monica in the morning since we now have an even happier reason to do so, Xander commented. Kim nodded. "I can't wait to see the shock on her face," Xander added. The two of them could not be giddier about their future, but most of all, their new addition to the family.

Chapter 5

Raven was to meet individuals regarding Eric's two offshore accounts. She took a ride-share to Amtrak to connect with both executives in Toronto, Canada. Being there in the station gave her pause after realizing it was the place where her son took his life. She was nearly overcome with sadness, but she pulled herself together quickly. She was on a mission now to get answers to Eric's death. This was not the time for her to fall apart.

Raven purchased her ticket earlier and had all the information she needed for the meeting. As she sat waiting for her train number to be called for boarding, she watched people hustling and bustling in and out of the station. Even though she seemed to be in a hypnotic trance, her mind was staying focused on the days' forthcoming event.

When Raven arrived in Canada, the people described greeted her. The two were dressed in very expensive attire and introduced themselves with straight faces. To Raven, they looked like the early 1920's Chicago Mafia. With no handshakes or smiles, they escorted Raven to a waiting limo.

After a short drive, the limo stopped in the downtown area in front of a beautiful glass building etched in gold trimmings with a tall logo statue prominently displayed. Walking toward the building, Raven watched the sunbeam's brilliant rainbow colors bounce off the large, gold-cased glass windows. She was taken to a glass elevator with an impressive view. The elevator stopped on the 15th floor, and they walked into one of the offices, where two other gentlemen were awaiting her arrival. One of them requested the documents that included Eric's death certificate and proof she was the heir to his estate. Raven pulled everything from her tote and handed it over. She was transferred to a different office to allow for a thorough review of each document.

In the anteroom, she was offered coffee, Danishes, and water while she waited. After about an hour and a half, one of the men came in to get her, and they returned to the main office. The top executive spoke, "Mrs. Raven Harris, we have reviewed and examined all documents presented to us. You are cleared to retrieve your son's package." Thank you, sir," she replied. This was a comfort to Raven. She breathed a sigh of relief, glad to know there would be no further hold-ups or any additional information needed. Please wait here while we get everything together. Someone will return and take you back to the Amtrak station. Raven nodded as all of the men got up from the table together, leaving her there in her thoughts.

The entire time there, all of them had the same ice-cold expression on their faces. Now, this is interesting, she thought as she sat there as instructed. The top executive returned minutes later with a tightly wrapped package and handed it to Raven. It had substantial weight, but she didn't care. She was just ready to get out of there as quickly as possible.

Two of the men rode the elevator with Raven back down to the entrance level and escorted her to a waiting limousine. On her ride back to the train station, she was more relaxed and was able to admire the beautifully constructed buildings in the business district. When she got to the station, Raven had a few hours before she would be boarding her train. She purchased a couple of magazines, a pack of peanut butter crackers, and a bottle of iced tea from the gift shop to pass the time away and engaged in small talk with some of the people while waiting.

Finally, the train arrived, and Raven was on her way back to Chicago. It was an exhausting and tiring day for her. She planned to see Marcus Blackstone once she returned, but she was too tired. All she could think of was taking a hot shower, having a little dinner, and getting some rest. She decided she would see him the following day, along with opening the offshore package. The day had taken a toll on her. Raven needed peace and quiet for now. She nodded off periodically on the long ride back, but was sure to keep the package close to her.

The conductor of the train came walking down the aisle, announcing the station in Chicago. Raven wipes her eyes, puts her magazines in her tote, and stands up straight. While exiting, she texted for a Lyft ride-share, which took no time. She quickly arrived at the Wilshire Hotel and walked to the front desk to extend her stay. While taking the elevator up to her room, she changed her plans and decided she would have dinner and a drink in the lobby hotel restaurant.

She put everything down in the room, including the weighted package from Canada, and went back down to the restaurant. Raven was seated by a waitress and handed a menu, stating she would return in a few minutes. There were many choices to choose from. Raven only wanted something light with a glass of wine and the relaxation of the atmosphere. To wind down from her excursion earlier in the day is what she needs right now. The waitress returned and took Raven's order of baked salmon atop a fresh green salad and a glass of white wine.

As she indulged in her meal, Raven overheard guests at the next table talking about the upcoming wedding of Kimberly Casey and Xander Carlisle that was occurring in two days. She carefully listened as they talked about her son and Kimberly, the horrible outcome of his attempt on her life, and the happiness she found afterward. Everyone at the table spoke highly of her, as though she were a queen or someone important. Truth be told, she was considered high society in Chicago, and that was all because of her work and community involvement. Raven wanted so much to yell out to all of them, but she held her composure. She finished her wine, signed the check, got up from the table, and left the restaurant in haste. It appears no one paid any attention as she hurried out.

Raven was nearly out of breath when she opened the door to her room, nearly hyperventilating. She opened the hotel fridge, grabbed one of the small bottles of water, and took a sip to calm herself. You'd think she would have gotten used to hearing negativity about Eric by now since it had been a while, but instead, she was reliving it each time there was any mention of him.

Leaning on the counter, she thought of the ring found in his safe deposit box and wondered if it was intended for Kimberly. "What happened?" was the question she kept asking herself. To figure out what led to her son's abrupt collapse into chaos, Raven needed to put the puzzle pieces together. She hoped she would get more answers from Marcus when she visited him the next day.

Raven looked up and stared at the package in the chair. She was going to open her son's package when she returned to her room, but the day was a little too hectic, so she decided to hold off. Raven, unconcerned about further surprises, stored the package in her closet, took a warm shower, and retired for the evening.

Chapter 6

Kim and Xander rethought their decision to tell Monica about her pregnancy at the office but instead invited her and her husband Jay to dinner at their new home. While Xander fired up the grill for the marinated ribs and Kim prepared the baked beans and green salad, she expressed her concern about how Monica would react to the news of the added work responsibilities.

In his Al Green voice, Xander sang, "Everything's Gonna Be Alright," and they both, at the same time, burst out laughing in triumph. Humming and rocking from side to side, Xander turned around to check the meat on the grill. Silently, Kim continued to ponder how Monica would manage the business while being off her feet for the next few months. Xander continued to reassure her that Monica would be happy for them and would do her best with additional tasks and duties, and he would expect nothing less. Kim nodded. She knew Xander was trying to ease her mind, but there was still concern that she might think it would be too much for her.

Everything was prepared and ready to eat. After creating a beautiful and elegant table, Kim dashed to her bedroom to finish dressing. Just as she entered the bedroom, she heard the musical chime of the doorbell. Monica and Jay were right on time. With the sun brightly shining through the sliding patio doors, it felt like a great day to dine with close friends. Xander let the couple in, took their coats, and gingerly hung them in the coat closet. Did you have trouble finding us? "No, not at all," the GPS brought us right to your door, Jay replied.

With delight, they followed Xander into the beautifully decorated entertainment room with recess lighting, a chandelier, and tabletop lamps. The combo media, gaming, and bar room have a unique style and design. It features a home theater screen with surround sound and a modular dark blue velvet sectional with a marble-top bar encased with mahogany cabinets with glass shelves.

Being the host, Xander offered them drinks from the bar. They were in awe of the room itself and amazed at the décor and the design. They complimented Xander on the ambiance in the room. He admitted that he and Kim together chose the furniture and the décor, but that it was her expertise in interior design that really set the tone. Jay commented while looking around and sipping his mojito cocktail, "You both have great taste," and Monica agreed, nodding. Xander thanked them for the compliments.

As they continued to engage in conversation, Kim walked in and gave her guests each a hug and Xander a kiss on the cheek. Monica noticed a glow about Kim but kept the comments to herself. They listened to music and mingled for a while longer before dinner was served.

Dinner-serving platters, trays, and large bowls were set on the table. White wine was served with dinner. Kim filled her wine glass with seltzer water, not wanting to give herself away to her guests. "Man, these ribs are great!" Jay said. The sauce is spot-on. Where did you learn to grill? Xander laughed out loud and replied, "I do alright in the kitchen." Well, whatever the case, you can come to our house any time you want and cook up some more of these. Jokingly feeling left out, Kim pouted, "What about my beans and salad?" They all laughed. Monica said, "Of course, everything is wonderful." Thank you so much for inviting us. Next time, dinner will be at our house. "It's a deal," Xander replied.

As they all wiped sauce from their faces, laughing, talking, and drinking the wine, Kim announced that she had something important to tell them. Everyone got so quiet; you could hear a pin drop. Xander got up from the table, went to Kim's side, and put his arms around her. "Xander and I are having a baby," she quickly said. Monica opened her mouth wide, smiling, but before she could say anything, Jay got up and said out loud, "Congratulations, you two," as he shook Xander's hand. Monica chimed in, "This is wonderful news! I am so happy for you guys!" I also have a secret to tell you. I noticed a glow on your face when you walked into the room earlier, but I didn't want to embarrass myself and ask. Kim and Monica laughed loudly as the two men stared at them. Sarcastically, Monica said, "It's a woman thing."

Xander interrupted their amusing conversation and took Kim's hand, saying, "Monica, we need to ask you a favor." "Anything, anything at all. What can I do?" Kim answered, "I need you to handle the office's day-to-day operations for the next few months." The doctor explained to us that I needed to take some time off and stay off my feet as much as possible. Xander and I thought you would be the ideal person to keep an eye on things, of course, with his help. Monica replied, "You don't even have to ask." In fact, I would have felt useless if you hadn't.

One more thing: Kim commented. As you know, Danielle is my matron of honor, and she usually goes with me to the dress fittings. To keep her from asking questions, would you please go with me tomorrow to do my final fitting? My dress is feeling a little tight, and I believe it will need to be let out a little.

Furthermore, I will tell Danielle and my staff about the pregnancy after the wedding. We also planned to tell our parents before they leave. That will not be a problem, Monica replied. My lips are sealed. Great! Now, are you sure about handling the office for a while? Girl, I gotcha'. Everything will be fine. With the two of you in and out, we won't miss a beat, Monica assured her. Thank you so much! I really appreciate it, Kim commented. Feeling relieved, they exchanged smiles and hugs.

Chapter 7

Raven got up and ordered breakfast with coffee and juice. She took a quick shower and dressed before her food arrived. She opened the door for the morning paper and sat down to read while drinking a small bottle of water. Nothing interested her on the front page, including the continuing coverage of the wedding of Kimberly Casey and Xander Carlisle. Apparently, it would be the most fabulous event of the year. Glancing at the bottom of the page, the article mentioned the revealing of Ms. Casey's dress, the dressmaker, and how the media would be there for the event. Raven cringed at the thought of it all.

A knock at the door startled her out of her hideous reverie. It was room service with her breakfast. She nearly lost her appetite, but knew she had to stay nourished and energized in order to face Marcus Blackstone in prison later today. Putting her mind at ease, she sat down and enjoyed over-easy eggs, sausage, grits, and toast. After finishing, Raven had to admit to herself that the food was absolutely delicious and satisfying. She continued sipping her coffee as she scanned more of the paper for Broadway shows and clothing sales to pass the time until she was ready to go out for the day. She circled a few things she wanted to return to later.

Bored, Raven got up to enjoy the view outside the large window of her room. The sun loomed over the horizon as it was rising. What a beautiful sight, she thought as she wrestled to put a smile on her face. The more she watched the breathtaking view, the more Raven began to feel calm and relaxed. She stood there for a long time before finally breaking away to begin her day.

Raven grabbed her purse and went down the elevator to take an Uber to the Chicago Penitentiary. When she walked in the prison, the smell was horrendous, a far cry from the pleasant atmosphere of her hotel room. She walked to the reception window, where there was a jailer, and asked to see Marcus Blackstone. The jailer asked who she was and if she was a family member or not. Raven responded, "I'm a friend; he was like a son to me when he was a child." I am visiting Chicago and heard he was here. I'm sure he would like to see me. "Wait here," the jailer replied as he got up and walked away from the window. Raven was feeling a little nervous inside, but she needed to see him.

Regardless of how she felt about Marcus, she wanted answers about her son, and he was the one person who could probably give her the most insight and information about him. Raven sat there for nearly an hour contemplating the questions she needed to ask Marcus before the jailer returned and nodded to her. She was directed to a set of steel doors to walk through. She was thoroughly checked with an electronic surveillance instrument from head-to-toe by a female officer for contraband, metal items, or anything that would deny her entry. She started to feel violated and dirty, but she took it all in.

When Raven was cleared, she was escorted to a chair in front of a polycarbonate glass partition with a phone attached to the right side of the wall, separating her from the opposite side. She was then instructed to sit. A few minutes later, Marcus was escorted into the room, his handcuffs removed, and directed to the chair in front of Raven. The officer then stood back a few feet while he talked with her.

Marcus looked shocked to see Raven for a moment before picking up the phone. She then picked up her end of the phone. Marcus, with a confused look, spoke first. "Ms. Harris, I was surprised when they told me that you, of all people, were here to see me. What are you doing here?" "Hello, Marcus," she replied. I came here because I wanted some answers from you.

I watched a documentary about Eric on 20/20, which included accounts of his heinous crimes. When I heard that you were a part of it, I was not surprised at all. I told Eric years ago to stay the hell away from you, but I see he didn't heed my advice. What happened to my son, Marcus? Was he in trouble? If he needed help, why didn't he call me?

"It ain't nothing like that, Ms. Harris." Ugh... Eric was still hot with the ladies, living dat whore life and having fun. Until he met dat girl, he started to get cerious wit. Dat girl had his nose wide open. I don't know what happened, but she started to ghost him, and he got upset about it, and I didn't know why. I forgot her name, but she owned some kind of color painting business. I don't know what cha call it, but it's located in downtown Chitown. "You don't know what it was?" Raven asked, piercing her eyes at him. "No, ma'am, I don't," Marcus replied. I came on the scene long after he had known her for a while.

Wen someone got in his way, he called me up to take care of it. "Take care of it." Take care of what? Raven asked seriously staring at him. "Well, dare was this lady he had been screwing, and she was blackmailing him for money. A hell of a lot of money too! She got wind of da girl he was cerious about and wanted revenge for her time. Dat's what he told me, and he wanted to scare her into backing off of him. Bruh was determined he wasn't going to go down like dat, so he called me to handle it, to keep his hands clean. So, he paid you to do his dirty work? Raven questioned. Yeah, somein' like dat, Marcus nodded. "And here you are, alive and well, and my son is in the grave," Raven said as she teared up.

"Ms. Harris, I had nonthin' to do with Eric's death." He did dat to himself" from what I hear of the whispers in here. "Don't blame me. You need to talk to dat girl!" Marcus said it in a harsh voice. I ain't that guy! Gritting his teeth in anger, I only did what I was paid to do before your son double-crossed me. He shot me, leaving me to die in the middle of de street. Den, he took the money from my bleeding body to help him get out of Chitown. I didn't know why he wanted to leave until I heard the rumors of what he did to dat girl. He was on the run from the police, and dat's all I got.

"Who is this girl that tried to blackmail my son?" Raven asked. Some chick who owns a gym; it's in downtown Chitown too. Hur name Dany somein', ah... Danielle, that's it. Ion know her last name doe. She was rough to handle, and, um... "I don't need the nasty details!" Raven snapped. I already know the story. Anyway, thank you for the information, as she was about to hang up.

"Wait, wait! Ms. Harris, "Can you do a brother a solid?" Marcus asked. "Boy, what do you want from me?" "I helped you, so can you help a brother out? Can ya put some greenbacks on my books? I'm kinda low, he asked. Raven exhaled and felt sorry for him. She promised to do so before she left the prison, and then told him to take care of himself. Raven ended with a harsh goodbye before hanging up the phone.

Chapter 8

Monica and Kim met at the bridal studio for Kim's final dress fitting. Girl, you know everyone is hyped about your dress! Everyone, that is someone, including the media, will be there. "I know, Kim said. It is so exciting! I cannot wait to marry Xander. He is truly the light in my heart. I thank the good Lord for him every day.

While talking, Kim checked in, and they took a seat until her name was called. He has been so sweet during all the planning and has been there for me every moment, especially since we learned about the baby. Speaking of the baby, I need to take my prenatal vitamins. "I'll get you some water," Monica stated. You sit there, and I'll be right back. She returned, and Kim continued. "Don't get me wrong, Monica. Xander loved me before finding out about the baby, but he has been protective of me more than ever since the incident. He will not let me go anywhere without him, and he calls periodically during the day to see if I need anything and if I am okay.

We are currently discussing hiring a live-in housekeeper before the baby arrives, and he has also brought up the fact that I still need another designer in the office, something that we discussed before the incident. I was swamped at that time, but now I may seriously consider it. Xander is working practically every day in the office, but does take some days to come home early to spend some quality time with me.

"Monica, how-did-I-get-so-lucky?" Kim said, smiling. She went on to say, "If and when I decide to start interviewing a designer," I would like for you, if you don't mind, to sit in. I know I have asked a lot of you, but I want you to be comfortable with the applicant too." "That won't be a problem," Monica replied, smiling. In fact, I'm loving being in charge for a while, she teased. The two burst out laughing. "Now, as far as a housekeeper, I am contemplating a live-in or a few days-a-week housekeeper. I am sure Xander will grill and run a fine-tooth comb on everyone we interview. He is not going to just let anybody into our house," Kim said. "I have no doubt. Well, you must give the man credit. He is being efficient, Monica replied, laughing. "Yeah, you're right," Kim agreed.

The bridal coordinator called Kim's name for her fitting. The two got up and walked to the private area with a dressing room. Kim changed into her chiffon-laced designer gown, and as expected, it was a tad bit uncomfortable. The seamstress double-checked before placing pins in the areas to let out. Fortunately, there were only a few centimeters here and there to be altered. The seamstress indicated it would only take a few minutes, so Kim decided to wait.

Patiently, Kim and Monica sat and chatted amiably about the wedding, the baby, and an array of other things. "Does Danielle have her dress?" Monica asked. Lord, yes! She picked it up a week ago. She is so thrilled; I have no doubt that she puts it on every day. I have seen it on her, and she looks gorgeous. "I'm sure she does, Monica interjected. "How do you think she will react when you tell her about the baby?" She asked. "Oh, now that's another conversation; however, I believe she will be happy for us," Kim replied. I'm sure she will have no problem babysitting at all.

Ah, I forgot to ask you, "How is Jay these days?" "Working hard, as usual. He appears to be more excited about your wedding than I am, Monica said, laughing. You would think he was the father of the bride. Snickering, Xander's brother, Zayden, is thinking the same way too! Kim said. They might just be the life of the party at the reception since they are both the Best Men.

In preparation for the wedding, Xander said he felt it was only fair because both of them were so helpful to him during my ordeal. He would not have it any other way. While we're on the subject, Zayden and his parents will be here later tonight. They're staying at the Wilshire Hotel. Instead of having a rehearsal dinner, we decided on a nice, quiet dinner with them at home. This will give us a little downtime.

Afterward, Xander and his brother will meet with Jay for the bachelor party, but of course, without girls. "I know, Jay reminded me," Monica asserted. Jay got them a room at the Congress Plaza for their little shindig. A few more of Xander's friends will be joining them. "He will be staying there for the night," Kim confirmed. "Yep, and Danielle and I will be here with you for a small bachelorette party," Monica announced. A party with just us girls' will be lots of fun too!

The seamstress came out with the dress for Kim to try on again to ensure the areas she altered were comfortable for her. She changed into her wedding dress and returned to the platform with three full-length mirrors to view herself, this time with her veil.

As she turned on the platform, she radiated a vision of loveliness. Monica was in awe as tears filled her eyes. "You look so beautiful, Kim!" Monica said excitedly. Xander is going to be star-struck. I know the media is going to be all over this. "Do you think Xander will like it?" Kim asked. "Girl, that dress is breathtaking!" How could he not?"

The seamstress helped Kim out of the dress to hand steam, press, hang on a hanger with a cardboard bust form, and then cover it with a designer's gown bag. "Your wedding is going to be one to be remembered. I'm sure of it!" Monica said with tears still filling her eyes. Smiling and tearing up too, Kim said, "Stop before I have makeup dripping down my face." Monica handed her some tissues, and then they both laughed and hugged each other tightly.

Chapter 9

As Raven left the Chicago Penitentiary, she thought about everything Marcus described to her about Eric. Throughout the Uber ride back to the hotel, everything seemed to become dark and dreary, even though it was bright and sunny outside. Those thoughts moved to her baby boy, the child she raised and protected most of his life, and the one she praised for his accomplishments. Because of some woman he cared for, Eric ended his life, and I was not there to say goodbye.

Tears fell from Raven's eyes as she reminisced about the times she shared with him. She dabbed the tears away with her fingers. She told herself this was not the end, at least for her. Raven wanted to speak with Kimberly Casey and knew the task would be difficult. She didn't know how she would make it happen, but she had to know the story of what happened between the two. In her thought process, Raven felt this was the start of Eric's issues prior to his death.

Once arriving at the hotel, Raven walked in and stopped at the hotel bar for a pick-me-up. While sitting there nursing her drink of Martel and thinking to herself, the bartender noticed the sadness in her eyes and asked if she was okay. She did not answer him right away. When she looked up at him, it was evident that something was wrong. Her face said it all. He asked if he could call someone for her. Raven told him that she would be okay and that she was just lost in thought. The bartender nodded and went back to polishing glasses.

The bartender watched her face drop into both her hands. He went to the kitchen for a moment, and when she looked back up, he was still polishing the glasses. She didn't notice when he went to the kitchen again and later returned with a sirloin steak, a baked potato, and broccolini. He sat the plate down in front of her.

Raven looked up, saying, "I didn't order anything to eat." The bartender replied, "You look as though you hadn't eaten in a while," as he handed her a linen napkin enclosed with utensils. Don't worry, ma'am; it's on me. Raven quietly responded, "Thank you," and slowly unwrapped the napkin, took out the fork and knife, placed the napkin in her lap, and then cut into the steak. She appeared to liven up, and life seemed to return to her face.

The bartender felt bad for her and continued to keep a close eye on her. He thought maybe she needed something else to drink, so without question, he brought her a glass of iced tea. Raven looked at him and nodded. He was looking out for her, as he would for his own mother or sister, and did not want to see her drink her sorrows from a bottle or be taken advantage of. After being there a couple of hours, Raven thanked him, left a hefty tip, and walked to the elevator to get to her room.

Raven entered the room, undressed, took a shower, and began to feel better. As she put her thoughts in perspective and was in somewhat of an upbeat mood, Raven decided she would do some sightseeing and go shopping the following day. She had been busy since coming to Chicago a few days ago. With the dissolution of Eric's businesses, going to his home for the final time, and visiting Marcus in prison, she was overwhelmed and needed to exhale. Shopping would do the trick, she thought.

After watching a few TV shows and the news, she took the paper where she circled items to remember and googled shop locations. Raven figured driving her vehicle would be too confusing to find everything, so she decided she would take Uber or Lyft to sit back, relax, and enjoy the view. Her eyes began to get tired from all the reading. She stretched her legs out on the sofa and fell asleep. Waking up in the middle of the night, she realized she was not in bed. Raven got up, pulled down the comforter, and slid into the soft bed for the remainder of the night.

Raven didn't sleep deeply, so the sound of a thump on the door startled her awake. She sat up, rubbing her eyes, and then got up and went to the door. When she opened it, she saw the daily newspaper lying in front of the door on the floor. After picking it up and walking back to her bed, she noticed the time was a few minutes after 8 a.m.

Raven initially wanted to have breakfast out this morning, but she was still a little tired from the day before. She decided to go ahead and order room service instead. After taking a quick shower, she put on a pair of jeans, a turtleneck sweater, and sneakers, then plopped down on the chair near the window.

As she waited for her breakfast, she watched the movement of the people on the street down below. Shortly, there was a light knock on the door, with a man's voice announcing room service. When she opened the door, there stood a man in a white linen jacket and black pants. He pushed the cart into her room. She thanked him and tipped him handsomely. Her light breakfast consisted of a croissant, fruit, and juice. She made herself a cup of coffee from the Keurig in her room. Looking at the clock, Raven called Bergdorf Goodman, a high-end designer store, for an appointment scheduled for 11a.m. and booked an Uber in advance. To pass the time away, she sat in the armchair near the window and continued to read the newspaper while glancing up and listening to a TV morning talk show.

While leaving the hotel, Raven ran into the bartender from the previous evening. She thanked him again for his hospitality to her the night before. He replied, "No, but thank you! I appreciate the tip, but you didn't have to." I know, but it was the right thing to do, she said. I was feeling down, and your generosity cheered me up. "Glad to do it; where are you headed?" he asked. Oh, and by the way, as he extended his hand, "My name is Jeff." Raven shook his hand lightly and said, "Well, Jeff, I'm going to do a little shopping before I leave Chicago. I'll be heading home to Detroit in a few days," she replied. "Well, enjoy your day. I'm working two shifts. That's the reason why I'm here so early." You too, Raven answered, as she headed for the revolving doors to her Uber.

As soon as she arrived at Bergdorf Goodman, a stylishly dressed service representative welcomed her. The service desk is located adjacent to an elegant bridal studio, designer clothing stores, and restaurants. When she walked into Bergdorf and looked back, in the entryway was a gigantic, round raindrop chandelier decorated in crystals and soft lighting, with oversized artwork adorning the walls.

Shortly afterward, Raven's personal shopper was called to the desk. They greeted each other, and Raven was given a list of the different departments in the store. The personal shopper assistant asked Raven, What area would you like to visit first? She said the clothing area would be her first choice. As they walked over to the clothing and accessories department, there were models walking around in the store, showcasing different name brand clothing and accessories. Talking to several models gave Raven an idea of what she would like to purchase.

After viewing so many choices, Raven chose a Versace La Medusa Small Handbag, a Jason Wu Floral Print Pleated Crepe Midi Day Dress, and an Adam Lippes Eloise Floral Print Midi Dress. In all, she spent a total of $5260.00 and nearly felt bad for doing so. Still, in essence, she could get whatever she wanted with the extra money she had received.

Following her purchases and walking out the doors to her Uber, Raven suddenly remembered she had not opened the package she received in Canada from Eric's business associates. Silently admitting to herself that in the beginning, the thought of it made her nervous, and she knew eventually she would have to open it. Somberly, she got into the Uber and headed back to the Wilshire Hotel for the evening.

Raven entered her room, took a shower, and dressed in her pink silk pajamas. She reached into the small refrigerator, grabbed one of the small bottles of red wine, and poured it into a glass for herself. Gradually, her body began to calm down, but her brain was in an intermittent state of wandering about her late husband and son and what more she could have done to save them. Ultimately, her brain began to synchronize with her body, and sleep was drawing near. Raven got into bed, relaxing and pressing her head deeper into the goose down pillow, casting all her cares for another day.

Chapter 10

Kim and Xander's wedding day is here. Monica and Danielle stayed with Kim overnight and brought their attire with them. It was better this way because both wanted to be there for Kim to assist her in getting ready for the big day. They enjoyed their girl's night with wings, chips, and non-alcoholic beverages, laughing at their jokes, and enjoying the movie "Girl's Trip." After the movie, they all went to bed in their designated bedrooms.

The next morning, everyone woke up bright and early. They were just as happy and excited as Kim. It seemed like they were bending over backward, trying to keep Kim calm and relaxed. Monica is doing more since she has vital information about Kim's condition.

The make-up artist and hair stylist soon arrived as scheduled. They brought sketches of the hairdos and makeup that Kim and Danielle approved a few months earlier. They were astonished to see the sketches on the display board resemble them. While Kim gets her hair done, others have things to do before the wedding. Monica's niece and nephew were to be the flower girl and ring bearer. She would handle the basket of flowers and the ring bearer's satin white pillow. Danielle is preparing a light breakfast of small croissants, sausage, coffee, and juice for all of them. She set the food on the table, and they sat, ate, and talked about the wedding and the reception. After completing their meal, everyone got busy for the day.

The wedding will take place at the Harold Washington Library Center. The Ushers, two of Xander's friends, were there to check with the wedding planner, lighting and sound engineer, caterer, and other staff to make sure everything was in place for the wedding and reception. He wanted his fiancé's day to be special and could not wait to see her as she walked down the aisle on the arm of her father.

Last night was calming and relaxing for Xander. He spent time with Monica's husband, Jay, and his brother Zayden, as they enjoyed a few beers, chips, wings, and nuts, watched a hockey game, and talked about the wedding. Xander surprised his brother with the news of Kim's pregnancy, and he was elated. Zayden expressed his love for him and Kim. "Now, I will have a sister," he said, and a niece or nephew to spoil. "Oh, no, you don't, not before me, little brother," Xander laughed. Xander also swore him to secrecy from their parents, as he and Kim planned to tell all of them after the wedding. Zayden put two fingers together and moved them across his lips, saying, "My lips are sealed," smiling like a Cheshire cat.

Mom and Dad are going to be so happy, Xander. "I hope so because I know I am!" Xander replied happily. The two brothers hugged with affection. Jay, standing aside, said, "Don't leave me out," and they grabbed him into the fold.

It's hours away from the wedding ceremony. Xander confirmed with Zayden that he had the ring. He would be responsible for attaching it to the ring bearer's pillow when they arrived at the venue. They shot-the-breeze for a few minutes, then started to get themselves prepared and ready for the event.

Both Xander and Kim's parents got ready at their hotels and prepared to meet at the venue. Kim, Monica, Danielle, and Monica's niece arrived first and entered the room prepared for the bride. Xander had thought of everything with the help of the wedding planner. Kim was the only one not yet dressed. Obviously, she was keeping her wedding dress a secret because she did not want the media to reveal it before the ceremony. Kim wanted them to be as surprised as everyone else.

Shortly after, her mother arrived, and the two hugged tightly. "I am so happy for you, sweetheart," Janie said with tears in her eyes. Xander is a great guy, and me and your father love him so much. "Oh, Mom, don't cry." Kim hugged her again. The make-up artist and hair stylist were here just in case something happened like this. "Thank goodness for you guys," Kim said. "We are used to it, the two said, smiling. Now let's touch up that make-up and hair and get you ready for the man of your dreams, young lady. Everyone in the room smiled affectionately and scattered to continue getting ready.

The minister later arrived, with Xander, Jay, and Zayden close behind. Looking around, Jay and Zayden were amazed at what they saw. Several gorgeous antique gold pedestal candle holders with candles flank both sides of the room. They illuminate the essence of love, peace, and harmony. The soft lighting and the soft harp music surrounded the room with a romantic ambiance. The aroma of freshly cut flowers boosted the spirit and soul of the environment. Together, the décor and atmosphere will unite family, friends, and guests for the exhilarating event to come.

Some of the guests had arrived and were either talking softly or sitting quietly reading the wedding program. Everyone who received an invitation RSVP'd for the event, including the mayor of the city, Chief Investigator Simms of the Chicago Police Department, and their wives. Everybody who was anybody attended this wonderful occasion.

The media and guests were not permitted to take pictures until after the nuptials, which is stated at the bottom of the wedding program. The Ushers were directed to make sure the bride and groom's instructions were complied with, particularly when it came to the media.

Everybody was seated as the pre-ceremony began. The mother of the groom was escorted to the right side of the venue and seated on the front row with her husband. The mother of the bride was escorted to the left side and seated on the front row while she waited for her husband to walk their daughter down the aisle.

The ceremonial music, River for You, began to reverberate throughout the building. Danielle, matron of honor, entered on the arm of Zayden, and later Monica on the arm of her husband Jay. They carefully took their positions. Slowly, the harp music blended into the song Canon in D as the flower girl began her walk down the aisle, throwing flowers from her basket, then seated herself. Behind her came the ring bearer, who carried a white satin pillow with the ring attached. He was ushered toward Zayden, who removed the ring from the pillow and then directed him to the seat next to his sister.

Subsequently, the moment of truth arrived. Kim and her father, James, arm-in-arm, stood in the darkened entryway. For their grand entry, the harp musician played All My Life, and everyone stood with all eyes focused on Kim. You could hear the

the low sounds of "Ooos and Ahhs", as they began to walk slowly down the aisle. Even Xander was in awe as he watched her come toward him. Kim was a picturesque sight in her off-the-shoulder flare and fit gown cascaded with beautiful lace and a detachable tulle cathedral train. Her hair, in an up-do style, was adorned with a matching veil. As she walked closer to Xander, her dangling crystal earrings twinkled as the sunrays from the windows bounced off them. She was a vision of loveliness, and everyone could see it. Smiles all around filled the room of over 200 guests.

When they arrived at the altar, Kim and her father smiled into each other's eyes as he kissed her on the cheek and whispered, "I love you, sweetheart." Then the pastor said, "Who gives this woman the right to be married today?" Her father said, "I do." James retreated and took a seat next to his wife.

Kim turned and stepped closer to Xander. With a loving expression, he assisted her up the two steps. Standing side-by-side, they reached out to each other and gently held each other's hands. Everyone took their seats. The pastor started the ceremony with a prayer. Afterward, he asked the couple to face each other and join hands as they recited their vows to one another. Xander looked into Kim's eyes, pledging his genuine love and affection for her and vowing to keep her safe and protect her for the rest of his life. Kim, shaking, pledged her love to Xander, vowing to honor and keep him for as long as she lived. Throughout Xander and Kim's exchange of vows, tears of happiness filled their eyes. Kim's mother looked on as she thought of how happy and courageous her daughter was.

With his voice cracking following the vows, the pastor expressed a short confirmation of love to the two, then requested the rings. Zayden handed Xander Kim's ring, placed it on Kim's finger, and repeated the ring exchange vow after the pastor. Kim followed suit as she placed Xander's ring on his finger. Lastly, the pastor spoke kind words to unify their union and pronounced them husband and wife. The pastor smiled and said, "You may kiss your bride." Shyly, Xander planted a big, juicy kiss on Kim's lips. They turned and faced their guests, and the pastor introduced them as Mr. and Mrs. Xander Carlisle. The entire room erupted with clapping and cheers of joy.

As they began to walk back down the aisle, they stopped, hugged each other's parents, and gave their mothers a single long-stem red rose. The couple continued their walk back to the entryway for media pictures. After a few minutes, the event photographer was able to take stage pictures of the bride, groom, wedding party, family, and cutting of the cake. It seemed like it took forever for the last picture to be taken.

Hastily, the couple and the wedding party went to their designated areas to change into more comfortable attire for the reception. Kim changed into a lace chiffon dress embellished with tiny flower appliques around the high-waisted bodice. The free-flowing dress accentuated her body in all the right places. Xander saw her as she emerged from the bridal room. Her natural beauty, which shone under the crystal chandelier captivated Xander. Smiling from ear to ear, he gave her an affectionate hug and a passionate kiss.

Finally, the announcement came that Kim, Xander, and the wedding party were about to enter the banquet hall and the guests cheered. As they entered the room, there was more cheering, clapping, and more oohs and aahs. Shortly, the music began to play, and Mr. and Mrs. Carlisle walked to the center of the floor for their first dance. The father-daughter dance followed the couple's first dance. The guests enjoyed both dances and were amazed at how smoothly they glided across the floor.

After the dances, the guests were seated, and a three-course dinner was served. During dessert, the wedding party toasts the couple with some serious and funny speeches. The guests laughed, clapped, and lifted their glasses in agreement. The rest of the evening was filled with dancing and socializing.

When the reception was finally over, the entire family was completely exhausted from all the mixing, mingling, and dancing with each other and the wedding guests. Before returning to their hotel, the parents said their goodbyes with lots of hugs and kisses and expressed looking forward to a quiet lunch with their children tomorrow at Cabra in the West Loop of Chicago.

Before the vendors left for the evening, as a form of appreciation, Xander handed the caterer, wedding planner, sound and lighting engineer, DJ, and photographer each an envelope that contained a hefty tip for a job well done, and thanked them for the excellent service. He would also be sure to extend the same to Kim's make-up artist and hair stylist as well.

Earlier, Xander asked the caterer to prepare a separate plate for Kim to enjoy later. She mingled often with their guests and never got a chance to enjoy the meal before her. The day was perfect for a wedding, and they had a great time with the many family members and friends who celebrated with them.

Chapter 11

Raven woke up thinking about the package she had not opened in the past two days. She could not understand what had caused her to unravel and avoid the inevitable. Today, she would be brave and open the package to reveal the contents. Raven got up and walked to her suite's Keurig coffee bar and prepared herself a strong cup of coffee. As she turned to walk toward the chair, her eyes captured a snapshot of the bag she was given with the package inside. She hesitated for a moment, but she knew deep down in her heart that it was time to reveal another part of Eric's life.

Raven walked over to the bag, put her cup down, and carefully removed the heavily secured brown paper package from it. It was wrapped several times with silvery gray tape. Raven tried to remove the tape with her hands, but it only bunched up tighter. She looked around the room for some type of sharp object, but could not locate anything strong enough. Raven is a woman known to not back down from anything, and this was no exception.

Finally, she called the front desk and requested a pair of scissors. The desk clerk replied that someone would be right up with them. A few minutes later, there was a knock at the door, announcing housekeeping. Raven opened the door and was given the scissors and the morning paper. She thanked the housekeeper and gave her a tip.

Afterward, she walked over to the package and began to cut the tape. It took several minutes to cut through all of it because the scissors kept sticking to the tape. She then tore away several more layers of the brown paper wrapping. Once she got it off, there was another taped box. Raven cut the tape and opened the box. It contained a royal blue velvet case with a key attached to the latch. Darn it! she whispered. "What the hell is in this package?" she asked herself. She removed the key, stuck it in the keyhole of the latch, and opened the case. Shocked, she found carefully wrapped stacks of hundred-dollar bills. She unwrapped one of the stacks of bills and sat there, gazing at them. Raven counted 500 hundred 100-dollar bills in the bundle. Altogether, there were 40 stacks totaling $2,000,000.

Raven couldn't believe her eyes. Her hands started to sweat, and she turned around, rubbing them together nervously, wondering what her son did to get so much money. She felt as though a drink would do her some good right about now. Instead, she placed the opened stack of bills on the dresser, slowly walked to a chair, and sat down, not believing what she had in her possession. "Eric, where did you get all this money?" she thought.

After the initial shock wore off, she went back to the package, removing the remaining bundles. There was a velvet divider with a big enough hole for her finger to fit in. She put her finger in the hole and lifted it out. With her mouth opened wide, there was a brand new 32-caliber gun and a box of unopened bullets. Raven sat down on the bed, removed the gun, and placed it beside her. Raven's hands began sweating profusely as her body tensed, and her breathing became short and fast. Talking to herself, what was he doing with a gun?

Raven had to figure out what was going on and what she was going to do. With all the money she received from the police, Eric's home safe, banks, and the briefcase found with him at the end, it was equal to Raven having several million dollars. It was nice to have so much money to take care of herself, probably for the rest of her days; however, no amount of money in the world could sway her from the focus of knowing what or who triggered her son's erratic behavior.

She went back to the dresser, grabbed the money with shaking hands, and threw it back into the case, locking it up. She was fortunate that there was an available safe in her room, so she placed it there for safekeeping. She now had to have something to calm her nerves, but it was still too early for an alcoholic drink on an empty stomach.

Raven called room service and ordered breakfast. In the meantime, she sat down to read the morning paper to occupy her mind with other things. The front-page story was about Kimberly Casey and Xander Carlisle's wedding. Further pages revealed pictures of the bride and groom, family members, dignitaries, friends, and interviews. Raven knew the affair would be huge but didn't think it would cause such a stir in the city. Ms. Casey was beautiful, she thought to herself, and so was the venue from what she saw in the photos. She tried to figure out how she would be able to approach Kim without her knowing her real identity. She thought about the same thing with Danielle Moore as well. The thoughts ceased when her breakfast arrived. She was still reeling from all the money revealed earlier, but that had to wait for now, she told herself.

As she was eating her breakfast, she wondered if she were to approach Kim under an assumed name—perhaps her maiden name, "Wilder." That would suffice. Maybe, to pose as a journalist for a popular magazine, she could make an appointment to see Kim and discuss her new life as a married woman. During the interview, she would ask questions about her past relationship with Eric, how she rose above the ordeal, and moving on to finding the love of her life. This was all she could think of doing now.

When Raven turned the page, lifestyle was written in bold letters. Xander and Kimberly Carlisle were the first names she noticed. She read that the couple lived outside the city in an extravagant suburban area, heavily guarded, due to prominent millionaires also residing there. With this information, she would begin by trying to see Kim in her office, since it wasn't far from the Wilshire Hotel. There was no other viable alternative for now.

Raven took a shower and drank another cup of coffee before getting dressed. She had no plans for the day and decided to take a walk around the city to get some fresh air and clear her head. Later, she would tour the art museum and have dinner with a drink that evening at one of the local restaurants in the area.

After a day of doing something free of deadlines, Raven figured it would do her a lot of good and keep her mind off the events of the past few days. There were plans to be made to get the answers she sought about her son, but today would not be the day. She would instead enjoy a day of leisure and free herself from any issues.

Chapter 12

Xander and Kim slept late this morning, still exhausted from their wonderful, glorious wedding day. Due to Kim's pregnancy, they discussed postponing their honeymoon until after the baby's birth. The doctor had advised Kim to reduce her daily activities and avoid prolonged standing and walking. Without a shadow of a doubt, Xander will be there to help her in any way he can, including making sure she follows the doctor's orders.

Although they would be meeting their parents and Zayden later for lunch, he still prepared Kim some soft eggs, toast, and juice because she was now eating for two. After breakfast, Xander reminded her to take the prenatal vitamins the doctor had prescribed. Additionally, he raised the fact that we have a doctor's appointment next week. Simultaneously, they both laughed out loud, realizing they would soon have a little one in their arms.

Xander planned to be at every obstetrician appointment and attend all Lamaze classes. He is going to be a hands-on dad before and after the baby is born. Smiling, Kim shook her head every time he spoke about his role in becoming a dad. It seems like they have so much to do in so little time. They were so excited and couldn't wait for their lives as parents to begin.

In two weeks, the contractor is scheduled to come and discuss with them the construction of the nursery, the theme, and the paint colors. Watching Xander, Kim could see he was physically and emotionally drained. She begged him to slow down and rest before he collapsed from sheer exhaustion. Even though he said he would, Kim knew otherwise.

After the pregnancy announcement, she will discuss with their fathers about his drive to get everything done before the baby is born. Just maybe they can encourage him to share the workload with other members of the office staff so that he doesn't have to worry about doing everything for her. She would cross her fingers, hoping and praying that he would listen and take heed.

Xander and Kim enjoyed a light breakfast before taking their showers and getting dressed for the family luncheon. Kim purchased some maternity clothes but didn't see the need to wear any of them today. Currently, she can still wear her loose-fitting blouses, elastic waist slacks, and cape-style jacket. Being a little chilly in Chicago, Kim's short cape jacket flares out from her body, so she won't have a problem zipping it up. The outfit she chose to wear will camouflage her little belly bump, and it will not give away their special surprise.

Their parents and Zayden took Uber to Cabra and met Kim and Xander there. Everyone arrived on time and walked into the restaurant together. Reservations had been made, and they were immediately seated. Kim decided she would invite Danielle to lunch in the next few days and give her the news. She and Xander desired to enjoy their surprise alone with family since this was their last evening together until the baby arrived.

While reviewing their menus, the Matre'd approached them and requested their drink orders. Before anyone could answer, Xander requested two bottles of Armand de Brignac Ace of Spades Brut champagne and water for the table. Sparkling water for me, Kim mouthed with nearly a whisper. Everyone seemed to be okay with his take-charge response and returned to their menus. Kim interrupted and requested a lemon wedge with her water. The Matre'd nodded.

Zayden put the menu up to his face with a strained expression as Xander side-eyed him. Jokingly, Zayden put his finger to his lips while quietly saying, Shhh. Xander couldn't do anything but smile as he reflected on the childish pranks they used to pull off on each other growing up. Zayden straightened his face, returned to his menu, and sat erect in his chair. The Matre'd returned with their waters and the champagne. He popped one bottle and poured everyone a glass except Kim.

Preparing for the big moment, she quietly moved the sparkling water with a lemon twist directly in front of her. The parents were so involved with the menu that they didn't notice. Afterward, the Matre'd excused himself and said he would return for their orders. Xander interrupted everyone from the menus and requested they raise their glasses because he had an announcement to make. He stood up and helped Kim from her chair. In unison, with all their glasses raised, Xander and Kim shouted, "We're having a baby!"

Everyone but Zayden jumped up to come around the table to congratulate the couple. There were hugs and kisses all around. Poor Zayden exhaled, and everyone laughed. Xander knew how much it took for him to keep quiet. Smiling, Xander hugged his best friend and only brother.

Then the questions started, "When did you find out? When are you due? Will it be a girl or a boy?" Kim laughed at all the questions and said, "Calm down; we found out a few days before the wedding and wanted to tell you first before anyone else. We did not want any of you to leave tomorrow without knowing. "Well, I, for one, my brother, am glad you did, Zayden said, laughing." Jokingly, Xander said, pointing at Zayden, "I had to pay this guy to keep quiet," and the two burst out laughing. Xander's father, Bryce, said, "And he kept his mouth closed?" "Now, that my son is a real surprise," and the table erupted with laughter.

The Matre'd arrived, taking their orders, but now they were all distracted by the exciting news of the baby and giving well wishes. No other patrons in the restaurant seemed upset due to the family's uproar. Even close-by patrons were excited and gave the couple congratulatory wishes. In fact, this news was now the "topic of conversation" for those patrons far away as the news spread throughout the restaurant. "This announcement deserves a second toast, Kim's father James said, so let's raise our glasses once more to the new Mr. and Mrs. Xander Carlisle and little baby Carlisle." Together, everyone said "HERE! HERE!" and there was clapping and smiling all around.

The family enjoyed their lunches and conversations with one another. They talked about the wedding décor, food, and music, but mostly about the arrival of their bundle of joy. Excitedly, the future grandparents teased about who would babysit the first summer of its life, the upcoming birthday parties, and what name they would want the baby to call them, while Xander and Kim looked on with love and affection.

After finishing their lunch, Kim thought to herself that since their baby announcement caused such a stir in the restaurant, Kim wanted to tell Danielle before the news came out. She leaned in and whispered to Xander that maybe they should have her over for dinner later this evening. He nodded in agreement.

Kim's mom, Janie, looked at her daughter and asked, "Honey, are you feeling okay? Is something wrong?" "No, mom, just a little tired." Well, your father and I will be leaving tomorrow, so we need to get back to the Wilshire Hotel and pack, and you, sweetheart, need to get some rest. The Carlisle's chimed in agreement. "This was an extraordinary weekend. and what a great time we all had," Kim's father, James, commented. "And we will all be together again once the baby arrives," Xander added as he hugged Kim. There were nods and smiles all around the table. Everyone got up from the table to leave and say their goodbyes.

Zayden mentioned having a few more days off and decided to stay in Chicago to see more of the city. "Good," Xander told him. You should come and have dinner with us later. We also invited Danielle, so she will be there too. "Cool," Zayden responded. I will return to the hotel with Mom and Dad and see you guys later. The family walked out the doors and lavished each other with hugs and kisses, echoing their goodbyes. Kim called Danielle once they were outside, and she was elated to get the invite.

Chapter 13

In a taxi on her way back to the Wilshire Hotel, Raven noticed Kim, Xander, and their families leaving the Cabra restaurant. She quickly asked the driver to pull over, just close enough for her to get a good look. He did as she asked.

Raven got out of the car and asked the driver to wait for her as she walked closer, but not too close to be noticed. She saw them having conversations as they smiled and hugged each other outside the restaurant doors. All the laughter made her quite sad and misty-eyed as she reminisced about the family she once had. After standing there for a little while watching, she walked back to the taxi, got in, and directed the driver to the hotel.

As Raven walked through the hotel doors, she walked past the bar, then stopped and turned on her heels to go and have a drink before going to her room. When she walked into the bar, she saw that bartender Jeff was on duty. They struck up a friendly conversation before he poured her a glass of red wine. Raven nursed the wine, taking a sip every now and then during their talk. Some of the conversations made her laugh, and other parts made her take notice of her surroundings. When she emptied the last drops of the wine and looked around, she saw the parents of Xander as they walked in. They sat down at the first available table.

Immediately, a waiter went over to greet them and introduced himself as their server. Bryce Carlisle responded, "Thank you, um...We would like two glasses of champagne. It's our last night here, and we're still celebrating our son and his new wife. They just got married yesterday, and today they invited us to lunch, surprising us that they're also having a baby! We are so happy for them and look forward to our new grandchild in a few months. "Well, I guess congratulations are in order. I will be right back with your drinks," the server replied.

Bryce and Madeline talked amongst themselves, awaiting their drinks, when Raven walked over to their table, interrupting their private conversation. "Hi, I don't mean to interrupt. I overheard you say that your son got married yesterday and you're having a grandchild soon. I just wanted to come over and say congratulations to you both." Madeline nodded and said, "Thank you so much." Her husband nodded looking on. There was a silence. "Hey, let me buy your drinks this evening," Raven quickly said. "No, that isn't necessary," Bryce replied. We're okay. "No, please, let me do this. It's been a long time since I've heard some happy news," Raven commented.

Bryce thought her to be slightly eccentric or drunk. At this juncture, to get her to move on from their table, he accepted. "Sure, that will be fine then," he said. Thank you again. Raven smiled and retreated to her seat at the bar. She waved to Jeff to let him know she would be paying for the couple's drinks and responsible for their tip so that he would relay it to the server. Jeff responded, "Okay," and returned to completing his customers' drink orders.

After the second glass of wine, Raven paid for all the drinks and tips, grabbed the small bags she came in with, and left to go to her room. When she got there, fury crept in. "So, they're pregnant too!" she said out loud to herself. She returned to feeling sorry for herself, and then vengeance washed over her as she shook her head angrily. "She is having a son or daughter, and my only child is gone because of her, and probably that husband of hers too," she thought. Feeling the way she did, Raven pulled out her computer, googling again for the phone number of Kim's studio. She was more adamant than ever to get to the bottom of Eric and Kim's relationship. When she found it, she wrote it down and told herself that she needed to calm down. She got a bottle of water from the hotel fridge, sat down, and turned on the television as a distraction from this new revelation. The day had gone so well until she heard the news of Kim and Xander's baby.

As she drank the water, Raven wiped away tears. She started to feel sick and got up to take a shower. After a warm shower, she put on her new short-sleeve silk pajamas and slid into bed. She still felt uneasy, but at least now her body was relaxed. Raven laid there for several hours, looking up at the reflection of the crystal lamp and listening to the muffled sound of the television, thinking that a new day was coming—a new day to get the answers she needed.

The next day would be Sunday, and Raven would focus on making plans for how and what to do with all the money she had in her possession. She also needed to call home and check with her brother Harold regarding the sale of her home. With her mind racing, she had so much to do but needed to settle down and prioritize her tasks and goals. All of the tasks seemed overwhelming, yet if she kept her mind on everything separately, everything would all work out, she thought. Nevertheless, one thing she cannot forget is the baby. The news pierced her heart and left Raven with sadness and pain deep down in her soul. This is all she could think about as she slowly drifted off to sleep.

Chapter 14

While Xander fired up the grill for salmon and asparagus, Kim laid down to rest before dinner. He carefully seasoned everything and placed a bottle of wine, champagne, and sparkling ice water to chill. They purchased cheesecake with strawberry topping for dessert on their way home from the Cabra restaurant.

About two hours later, Kim woke up to a delicious aroma drifting from the grill. She rubbed her eyes, looked at the clock on the nightstand, and slowly dragged herself out of bed. A little nauseous and out of sorts, she gathered herself, picked out an outfit, and headed for the shower. In the relaxing, warm water, Kim reminisced about the baby's room and the future of becoming a loving and nurturing mother. Suddenly, she was jolted out of her dreamlike state, remembering that it was almost time for Danielle and Zayden's arrival. Oh my gosh, I'll be so glad when I get through this first trimester, she whispered to herself. Morning sickness was taking its toll, and all she wanted to do was lie around and sleep. After tonight, that was the plan.

Xander came in as she finished dressing and saw how tired she appeared. "Are you okay, sweetheart?" he asked her with concern. "Yes, I'm fine. "It's just that this morning sickness gets the best of me sometimes," Kim replied. "I hate seeing you suffer like this, sweetheart. Is there anything I can do? Do you want me to cancel dinner?" he asked. Oh no, honey, I'll be fine in a few minutes. You have cooked a wonderful dinner based on the aromas I could smell. The shower was refreshing and helped a lot.

"Have you given any more thought to getting a housekeeper, just to be here in case of an emergency, at least until after the baby comes?" he questioned. "Yes, I have. Let's do it," she nodded. Maybe we can get started by surfing the internet, he said. That sounds like a winner, Kim said, trying to put a smile on her face. I'll look into it next week. In the meantime, let's get prepared for Danielle's reaction to our news. They laughed profusely.

Xander put on some soft music while Kim set the table in the dining room. As she put the gold-rimmed China place settings in front of each chair, she reminisced about the last time she used them. It was the first night she and Xander conveyed and consummated their love and affection for one another.

The joy of the memory put a smile on her face. When they finished, they both ended up back in the kitchen. Xander asked, "May I have this dance?" Kim replied, "Of course." They engaged in a slow dance, kissing each other and enjoying the music from the entertainment room.

The chiming of the doorbell disrupted their flirting, teasing, and laughter. Simultaneously, Zayden arrived in an Uber and started walking toward the door. A second later, Danielle drove her car around the Uber driver and parked in the driveway. Danielle was all smiles when she got out of her car. She was closer to Kim than ever before. Zayden hugged his brother and Kim as he entered, and Danielle followed suit. Man, this place is nice, Zayden replied. I know the décor was all done by my sister. I can see her all over it. Kim looked affectionately at her new brother-in-law for his comment about calling her his sister. He saw her expression and looked at her, saying he couldn't wait to say that.

"We love you, Kim, and I want you to know that you make my brother very happy, and that makes me happy too," Zayden said. Let's toast! Xander stopped him and said, "First, we have some news to announce," as he took Kim's hand. "What is it?" Danielle asked as she looked at him, then at Kim. Both of them smiled at her and said, "We're having a baby, and asked if she would do the honor of being his or her godmother. Danielle, flustered with stretched eyes, tears rolling down her face, both hands over her mouth with a ceremonious reply, "YES! Yes, I will!" Kim grabbed her tissues to catch her tears. They then turned to Zayden and asked him to do the honor of being the godfather. Misty-eyed, Zayden replied, "I would be honored," and hugged both Xander and Kim. Danielle hugged them too. Then Zayden and Danielle turned to each other and hugged tightly, and there seemed to be a spark between the two. When they realized what was happening, they pulled away slowly, looking at each other with shy smiles. Kim and Xander didn't notice the awkwardness or the look between them, as they were hugging each other too.

Okay, let's dry all the tears and get to toasting, Xander said, sniffing. He popped the cork and poured everyone a glass, except for Kim, who had already filled her champagne glass with sparkling water with a twist of lime. As they began to lift their glasses, Xander interrupted and said, "Zayden, would you like to do the honors?" Sure, bro, Zayden said. Let's raise our glasses high. "I want to wish my big brother and my beautiful sister, smiling at Kim, the happiest life ever, and to my future niece or nephew, the future Carlisle, a wonderful life that comes with much love ahead." I would like to add something, Danielle said. "It took time for us to get here, and I am so thankful for this chance to be in the lives of people that I love most in this world. Congratulations, and much love from me too." All glasses were tapped with smiles.

They sat down to dinner with a prayer and more conversations about the baby. A garden salad was served first to get dinner started. Zayden shyly looked over at Danielle and smiled, and she returned the look. This time, Kim noticed and lightly hit Xander on the knee to draw his attention to them.

After dinner, Kim asked if anyone was ready for dessert, and in unison, everyone replied with a "yes." Xander popped the cork on the bottle of Selvagrossa "Ica" Marche Rosato '21 wine and gently poured it into each of the goblet wine glasses. Kim filled her goblet with cranberry juice. Smiling, Xander said, "It looks like you were prepared for this day." Kim smiled back and continued to fill the dessert dishes with the cheesecake, while Xander placed them on the table. The room was filled with love and happiness as they talked about the wedding and, of course, the baby.

Kim gave Danielle a tour of the house and the room, which would soon be decorated with a baby theme. Xander and Zayden went to the entertainment room to listen to music and talk about guys' stuff. The evening ended on a high note with lots of hugs, kisses, and goodnights.

As Kim and Xander were closing the door, they noticed Zayden was walking Danielle to her car. They believed it was a sweet, wise, and gentlemanly thing to do. Even though Zayden is a true gentleman, he had other reasons why he walked with her. As Danielle began to get into her car, he stopped her and reminded her of the spark between them earlier. Zayden said, "I don't know if you are involved with someone or how you feel about a long-distance relationship, but I would love to see you again before I leave Chicago in a couple of days." I would like that, she replied, nodding.

"Is breakfast tomorrow morning too soon?" Zayden asked. "No, I would love to have breakfast with you," Danielle agreed. "Great! I'm unfamiliar with the Chicago area, where do you suggest we meet?" he questioned. "Let me check some places and give you a call in the morning," Danielle responded. Laughing, Danielle asked, How do I get in touch with you? Laughing with her, Zayden said, That's a good question. At that moment, they pulled out their cell phones and exchanged numbers. Zayden opened the door for her as she got in and rolled down her window. "If it's okay, I will give you a call about 8 a.m.," she commented. That will be fine, he said with a smile. Danielle raised her eyebrow, put her car in reverse, waved at him, and backed out of the driveway. Zayden will be staying with Xander and Kim for the remainder of his stay in Chicago. For that reason, Kim had already prepared a guest room for his short visit.

Chapter 15

After the evening with Kim and Xander, Danielle was so tired and worn out. She removed her clothing, walked into the bathroom, lit a candle, and ran herself a warm lavender-infused bubble bath. The thought of seeing Zayden again added more warmth as she sat and absorbed the light, fresh, flowery aroma. When she leaned back in the tub, the scent reminded her of a glimmer of hope that lay deep inside her soul. Finally, she was able to face her demons and move on. After thirty minutes of relaxing, she put on her nightgown, got into bed, and fell sound asleep.

As the sun rose the next morning, as promised, Danielle called Zayden with the restaurant details. He answered on the first ring. It was obvious that the two could not wait to see each other again. They both rushed through their morning rituals and affectionately greeted each other with big hugs and smiles before entering the Sunny Side Up Breakfast and Lunch restaurant.

They sat down at a cozy corner table and ordered croissants, omelets, potatoes, burritos, and other high-carb foods. As they sipped mimosa, their eyes sparkled as they momentarily gazed into each other's eyes. Comfortably, they talked about different landmarks in Chicago, the weather, and their favorite hobbies. The more they talked while enjoying breakfast, the closer the two seemed.

Danielle was amazed at Zayden's upbringing but a little embarrassed about her own. Zayden sensed her reluctance and saw the sadness on her face as she talked about her family and her life up to this point. Danielle's past after growing up was no picnic, and she disclosed very little. He changed the subject and asked her about her gym, Core's. Danielle's eyes brightened when she talked about wanting to help others lose weight, get into shape, and extend their livelihood. He did not expect her to talk about what occurred years ago. He had heard enough of it from Xander, and he didn't want Danielle to relive it all over again. Excitedly, she talked about all the renovations that had taken place in the last year and how much she loved her patrons. They smiled at each other as they talked about how beautiful Kim and Xander's wedding was and the dinner from the night before. Danielle was truly happy for them and said as much to Zayden. After the two sat back in their chairs from eating so much, Zayden suggested they take a walk when they finished eating.

When leaving, he took her by the hand as they walked through the east side of the Chicago Loop. It was soon time for Danielle to leave for work. Consuming those high-carb foods would keep her energized for the remainder of the day, Danielle thought to herself. She was booked with appointments from noon to 5 p.m. Respectfully, Zayden walked her to her car. They stood there awkwardly for a moment or two, then Zayden leaned in to kiss her. Like teenagers, they began to blush, giggle, and smile at each other. As he opened the door for her, she was reminded of their dinner date. Danielle looked at him, nodded her head, and smiled. She left the parking deck, and he walked back toward the restaurant while calling himself an Uber. As they both departed, Danielle and Zayden felt like they were on top of the world, in a state of euphoria.

Zayden walked into the house, smiling and talking to himself, with his mind focused strictly on his breakfast date. Not paying close attention, he bumped into Zander in the hallway. "Hey little brother, Xander said. You were up early this morning." We didn't hear you leave. "Yeah, I... um had breakfast with Danielle." Really? Xander asked sarcastically. "Yesssss, really," Zayden said enthusiastically. "The restaurant must have been crowded. It's afternoon," Xander commented. Laughing, Zayden asked, "What is this? Are you keeping up with your little brother now? I don't know if you've noticed or not, but this little brother of yours is all grown up." The two laughed, fist bumped, and hugged each other.

By the way, how is Kim? She's still having morning sickness, but otherwise everything is fine, Xander replied. That's good. Is she awake? I want to say hello to her. "Sure, but just for a few minutes. She is feeling a little under the weather," Xander replied. We're meeting with the contractor later about the construction of the baby's room, and I hope she'll be up to it.

Hey, will you be around for a while? I've got to run out for a minute, and I didn't want to leave Kim alone. Yeah, why? I only planned to take a nap for the next few hours, Zayden smiled. Thanks! If you get hungry, there are plenty of snacks in the cabinets. I'll be back in a little while. Okay, brother, thanks, Zayden replied.

"Oh, and by the way, I won't be here for dinner this evening. I will be dining with Danielle," Zayden inserted. "You are truly enjoying yourself these last few days, aren't you?" Zander quipped. "As the saying goes, time lost is time not spent, and I, my brother, am not wasting or losing any of it," Zayden commented. Laughing, Xander opened the door and left to go on a short errand.

Within an hour, he returned, surprising Kim with a large bouquet of red roses with baby breath. "Oh, my goodness, Xander, these are beautiful!" Kim said with her hands up to her mouth. You didn't have to do this. "You are my wife, and you are as beautiful as these flowers. I am going to show you how much I love you as often and as long as I live," Xander said with a twinkle in his baby-blue eyes. He walked toward Kim with a loving spirit and handed her the flowers, then hugged her with all his heart.

By this time, Zayden was awakened by Kim's excitement. When they saw him, Kim smiled and apologized for waking him up. "It's okay, what's going on?" he asked. "This sweet husband of mine went out and bought these lovely flowers for me. Aren't they beautiful?" "Xan, man, you are such a romantic," Zayden said, smiling and shaking his head.

The doorbell rang. Xander looked at the camera, and it was the contractor who was right on time. He asked Kim if she felt alright with meeting him, and she replied that she was fine. Xander let the contractor in and introduced himself, Kim, and Zayden. The contractor then introduced himself as Robert Norris of Norris Contracting Company. As he pulled out the plans for the room, he mentioned there would be two more guys assisting him in completing the job. Kim and Xander nodded with approval. Ahead of getting started, she offered Mr. Norris something to drink before they moved forward to review the plans, and he responded, "Water will be fine." Xander did the honors of retrieving a bottle from the fridge. At the same time, Zayden excused himself and retreated to the bedroom.

Mr. Norris had been given the dimensions in advance, so he was prepared and ready to present his proposal. Everyone sat down to review the plans, and he explained the layout and all the pricing for the project. Xander and Kim were impressed with everything they saw in Norris's work. It was understood Kim would create the décor for the room, and Norris's company would only be responsible for the construction, which include the windows, flooring, painting, and all the cleanup. Xander and Kim looked at each other with excitement.

Xander turned to Mr. Norris and said, "When can you start?" As soon as possible, Robert replied. We have a family member with us this week, so would next Monday work? Xander also explained that Kim is pregnant, so he would prefer they work after noon each day until the job is completed. Robert nodded, stating he understood. "So, do either of you have any questions for me?" he asked. Kim and Xander looked at each other, smiling, and nodded. "No, I think that's just about it," Xander replied. "I'll leave a copy of the plans with you, and if you see something you may want to change, please do not hesitate to contact me. "Here is my card," Mr. Norris said as he handed it to Xander. They got up from their seats and shook hands as they walked Norris to the front door. "We will see you next Monday, Mr. and Mrs. Carlisle," he said, walking to his truck. Xander closed and locked the door, then helped Kim back to their room to rest.

"I can tell the baby's room is going to be beautiful, don't you think, Xander?" she asked. "Yeah, Norris seems to know what he's doing," he commented. Now, all we need to do is find a housekeeper. "Right!" Kim nodded as she got into bed.

Chapter 16

Raven woke up fresh and ready to take on the day. She had now been at the Wilshire Hotel for a couple of weeks and knew the hotel's routine, but her thoughts returned to Carlisle's news of their son, Xander, and his wife, Kim, and her baby. She also knew they were staying at the same hotel and remembered they were leaving today after overhearing their conversation the evening before.

Raven sat up on the side of the bed and called her brother, Harold, for an update about the sale of her home. He told her that there were a few prospects, but no one had been approved yet for the sale. He said it would probably be any day now. Harold asked if she had completed Eric's business and when she would be returning home. Raven confirmed that she was done and that she was going to stay for a few more weeks to see the city. To ease his mind, she told him she would be home soon, not to worry, and that everything was fine. Of course, he was going to worry. Still skeptical, Harold continued to have questionable feelings about Raven being away for so long, but the sound of her voice being so upbeat did give him some comfort that she was okay.

Raven continued to sit on the bed for a few more minutes with the TV remote in her hand. She turned on the television to look at the local news before getting up to get the paper. Although she didn't have an appetite, she knew protein would give her the boost she needed to get through the day. With that in mind, Raven called room service and ordered two boiled eggs, toast, and juice, then prepared herself a cup of coffee from the coffee bar.

As the coffee brewed in the Keurig, she could hear the newscaster talking about a tip received in the newsroom late last evening about the baby news of Kimberly and Xander Carlisle. He continued, "We have reporters checking into it and hope to have more on the story on the evening news." Damn it! It's true, Raven said out loud. Why is it that she gets so much positive press, and they are hell-bent on continuing to trash Eric and destroy his reputation?" She grabbed the remote in anger and channel surfed until she reached more family-oriented programming.

After her breakfast arrived, Raven consumed half of the juice, a piece of toast, and one egg. The earlier broadcast had upset her, but she was determined not to let it spoil her day. She was in good spirits and decided to take a shower and dress. At the same time, Raven was determined to call Kim's office. She picked up the phone and punched in the numbers. Monica answered the phone, "Good morning, Designs, etc." Raven quickly asked to speak with Kim. "I'm sorry, Mrs. Carlisle is not in the office. May I help you?" Monica replied. "I want to set up a meeting with her to discuss creating a piece for me," Raven stated. I'm sorry, Ms..." Monica paused awkwardly. "Mrs. Wilder, Raven strongly voiced. "Yes, um... Mrs. Wilder, I'm sorry, but Mrs. Carlisle will not be taking any design requests for the next few months. "You may want to check with other designers in the area," Monica recommended. "Well, to be honest, I was told that she was the best, but since she's not in for a while, I'll check back later," Raven calmly said and immediately hung up. Of course, she wasn't in. She's somewhere enjoying her life! Raven angrily mumbled. She calmed down, finished the last of her juice, gathered her toiletries, and headed for the shower.

While dressing, Raven was thinking and decided to visit that gym girl's place, which is the name she called Danielle's Core Gym. If she wanted to look workout worthy, she would need to get some workout gear to appear as a general fitness client. Pulling out her laptop, Raven searched for places that sold activewear. To be certain Danielle would be there, she called the gym and was told she would arrive around noon. That would give Raven plenty of time to shop for something appropriate. "Great! Raven replied. I'm new in town and want to talk with her about touring and possibly joining her gym." "I can set you up with someone else here who would be glad to assist you with that." Would you like me to schedule an appointment for you?" the desk clerk asked. "No, no, I would rather see the owner, if that's not too much trouble," Raven commented. "Not a problem; I can do that." How... How does 1:30 sound? she asked. "Sure, that will be fine," Raven replied. "Your name, please?" "Mrs. Wilder," Raven said. "First name?" Does it matter? Raven bluntly asked. "No, ma'am, not really; it's okay. Not to push her any further, the clerk nicely said with a smile in her voice, "Okay, I've got you down for 1:30 p.m., and we'll see you then, Mrs. Wilder." "Fine," Raven said in an annoying voice, and she forcefully hung up the phone.

After a few seconds of deep thought, Raven got back to the task at hand. Surprisingly, she quickly found a sports store and called for an Uber, requesting an ETA. The time was around 10 a.m., and the Uber was scheduled to arrive in the next ten minutes. Raven grabbed her purse, the expensive one she purchased on her shopping spree, put what she needed in it, and hurried to the elevator.

Uber was there, waiting. Raven got into the car and directed the driver to Bergdorf Goodman, where she looked through several matching outfits of activewear until she saw one that suited her. She chose a pair of high-waisted leggings with a matching top, a Meshed Up Ombre Hoodie sweater, sneakers, and a pair of socks. If times were different, she would have gone to Target or Walmart, but she was now living her best life.

Raven obtained the necessary items for presenting the farce and returned to the hotel to change. She had time left before her appointment, so there was no rush to get dressed. She called and scheduled her second Uber for the day. Raven was taking advantage of her stay in the Windy City. She was ready to go again and rushed downstairs in the elevator for her rideshare.

When she arrived at Core's Gym, Danielle was still in awe of her newly reconstructed office, armed with an alarm she could immediately reach in case of danger. She also installed security cameras throughout the inside of the gym and hired around-the-clock security to patrol the perimeter of the building. The protection was not only for her needs but also for the staff and patrons who frequented her establishment. Danielle wanted everyone to know that she cared about their well-being and that they could feel safe in the environment.

As scheduled, Mrs. (Raven) Wilder arrived at the gym and walked to the front desk. She was kindly told to have a seat and that Danielle would be with her shortly. The front desk clerk beeped Danielle's office phone to notify her that Mrs. (Raven) Wilder had arrived. Moments later, Danielle came out to meet Mrs. Wilder and took her to the office for a consultation before the tour. To get a feel for the type of person Danielle was, Raven was cordial and appeared interested in what Danielle described regarding the accommodations at her facility. She explained everything in detail: the gym's workout areas, group classes that included beginners to advanced workouts, yoga, and tai training. For those who required personal attention, personal training was available. "This all sounds interesting," Mrs. (Raven) Wilder commented. "Shall we take a tour?" Danielle professionally asked. "I would love that," Raven replied.

After completing the tour of the gym, Mrs. (Raven) Wilder and Danielle returned to her office for any questions she may have. When Danielle started to ask her, she was quickly interrupted. "You look familiar. I've seen you somewhere," Raven said, tilting her head and placing her first finger on the right hand on the corner of her mouth. Oh yes, she deceitfully said. Your picture appeared in a magazine I was thumbing through a couple of days ago. The article's focus was on the wedding of a distinguished couple here in Chicago. Danielle, blushing with a smile, said, "Yes, it was the wedding of my best friend." "Oh, I see," Raven replied. Without any hesitation, Danielle ended the consultation with follow-up questions. Danielle asked, "Mrs. Wilder, did you enjoy the tour, and do you have any questions for me?" Raven felt that since Kim and Danielle were close friends, she would not receive any information from Danielle, so to avoid coming across as nosey, she didn't press the issue. She is a stranger, after all. "No, I believe you've explained everything to my satisfaction, Raven replied. I think I would like to take some time and try out some of the cardio machines. If that's okay with you?" "Certainly, would you like some assistance?" Danielle questioned. "No, I think I'll be able to handle myself. If I run into a problem, then I'll ask for help," Raven said. "Good," Danielle replied as she got up and extended a hand to her. Thank you for coming to Core's Gym, Mrs. Wilder, and if you decide to join, please feel free to talk with someone at the front desk, and they will get you all set up. Have a great day, and we hope to see you again soon. "Thank you," Raven said as she opened the frosted glass door and left to go out onto the floor until she reached the area of the treadmills.

While working out on the treadmill for nearly thirty minutes, thoughts of how she would be able to approach Kim deepened. She needed a strategy and a little help from someone or something. "What was her life like before she met my son? Who was she with before him? Was she ever married?" These were the thoughts running through Raven's mind. Then she had an epiphany. "I'll get an investigator to do a complete background check on her; that's what I'll do!"

When Raven completed her workout, she called for a ride-share. She thoroughly enjoyed her time at Core's Gym. It gave her the time she needed to think and make mental notes of the action to be taken. When she returned to the hotel, the first thing on her list was to find a reputable private investigator.

Chapter 17

For a few weeks, Kim had been experiencing difficulty sleeping. She was up most of the night, in and out of the bathroom. Kim was now appreciative of her doctors' recommendation to eat foods high in carbohydrates and to get plenty of rest. Watching Kim go through this phase of pregnancy broke Xander's heart. He fulfilled all of her requests and did everything within his power to help her, but he felt like it still wasn't enough.

Finally, Xander asked if she needed him to call her doctor, and Kim tried a little humor. "Honey, come and sit here, she said in a childish voice. Do you remember what the doctor said? "The first trimester might be filled with a range of uncomfortable physical and emotional symptoms as the baby starts to develop in my body, and most of them will dissipate in about thirteen weeks," Kim replied. We're almost there, and things should calm down in a few weeks. I think I can hold on until then. In the meantime, please bring me a piece of dry toast, water, and my vitamins. Appearing nervous and panicky, Xander said, "Sure." Within a few minutes, he rushed to the kitchen to retrieve the things Kim had requested.

Since experiencing morning sickness, Kim is a little concerned that Xander is overextending himself. Both of their fathers tried to reassure him that he would be just fine. They advised him to take a deep breath occasionally and to slow down. Kim knows Xander is doing everything to protect her, as well as trying to make her feel better. Frankly, it is apparent to her that he is struggling more than she is.

Xander returned with the warm toast, a bottle of water, and her vitamins. To calm him, Kim reminded him of the idea of hiring a "housekeeper," and he perked up. "Aren't there some services we can contact?" Xander questioned. I think so, she replied. He fluffed up her pillows to ensure she was comfortable in the bed before leaving the room to call Monica.

Xander dialed Monica's private line. She knew it was Kim or Xander, which made her heart palpitate for a second. He explained to her that he would not be in and to call him if there were any problems or issues. Monica said calmly, "Everything here will be fine. You keep focusing on and taking care of Kim, okay?" Xander responded, "Most definitely," as he attempted a smile. They said their goodbyes and hung up. Even though he tried to comfort Kim and himself, his concern about her morning sickness seemed to continue to loom over him.

When Xander returned to their bedroom, he looked at Kim and was relieved to see her propped up against a few pillows. The toast seemed to help Kim with the nausea, and she started to look better. She smiled at him and asked for her computer so they could begin searching for housekeeping services. He grabbed her computer and sat up next to her on the bed. "We should confirm the individual has some experience in first aid and can cook in the event something happens and I'm not here," Xander commented. Good idea, Kim said.

While they surfed the internet, Kim's phone rang. It was Danielle checking in on her. Kim smiled and thanked her for doing so. She explained that they were in the process of finding her a housekeeper. "I understand, and that's great!" Danielle commented. Well, I'll let you guys get back to it. I figured that I would give you a call before my next class, but I can talk to you later. "Okay, but do you need to talk now?" Kim asked. No, it can wait. I will talk to you later, Danielle said. Then she hung up. "I think she wanted to talk to you about my brother." Xander smiled. Probably so, but anyway, "let's get back to it," she requested. The two of them laughed.

After searching for hours, time seemed to fly by. The time was well after noon, and Xander was famished. He was so worried about Kim earlier this morning that he didn't think to cook himself breakfast, and now it was lunchtime. Kim agreed to have a cup of chicken noodle soup with some saltine crackers. He prepared what she requested and made himself two turkey sandwiches, opened a bag of chips, and had a Coca-Cola. He brought everything prepared on a silver tray given to them as a wedding gift so they could share as they looked over and discussed the list of housekeeping services prepared earlier. They decided to contact two of them after finishing their meal.

Xander took the tray to the kitchen and returned to make some calls. Neither service had anyone who had what they required.

Subsequently, Kim said, "Maybe we should place an ad and be specific so that we don't get an unqualified and incompetent housekeeper. "That probably would be best; this way we can both interview them," Xander replied. "Okay, I will write the ad, and you can proofread it so that we agree and are clear on what we're looking for before placing it in the paper tomorrow," Kim said. We should also specify a cut-off date for taking applications and set aside at least two to three days for interviewing those we feel are qualified, rather than interviewing here and there. I'll put together an application. Cautiously, they both agreed to interview at the office instead of at their home. Xander interjected, and I also prefer meeting with the applicants on a Saturday. He wanted to be careful for her sake as well as his own. Great idea! In a week or two, I will be in my second trimester and should be ready to interview applicants. Xander nodded and agreed with her.

As Kim began writing the ad, Xander went to the kitchen to prepare dinner. He seemed more composed than he had been earlier in the day. After seeing Kim up and about, his heart warmed, and he let out a big sigh of relief. Humming his favorite song, Xander put on his chef apron, seasoned his catfish, and placed it in the oven to bake. In addition, he heated the leftover chicken noodle soup and placed some saltines on a small platter for Kim, along with baked potatoes and salad for the two of them.

Kim finished the ad and decided to call Danielle. The front clerk requested that she hold a moment. Danielle answered, "Oh, hey girl, I wish that I could talk, but I have an aerobic session in five minutes. Tell you what, how about I come over tomorrow? I will take the day off, and we can spend girl time together and catch up." That will be fine. Xander is going into the office for a few hours, and he'll feel better knowing someone will be here with me, at least for a while, otherwise, he will be blowing up my phone, Kim said, and they both burst out laughing. Okay, great! I will see you tomorrow, Danielle spoke excitedly.

As Kim reviewed the ad again, making subtle changes, there was a knock on her door, and it was Zayden checking in on her. "How are you feeling, sis?" he asked. "Much better. I understand you have a dinner date this evening," she said. "Yep, Ms. Moore is doing me the honor of dining with me this evening," he replied. "Seems serious— two meals in one day?" Kim said, looking at Zayden with a smirk. Zayden laughed and said, It's just dinner. "Okay, brother-in-law. Can we expect you before midnight?" Kim asked. "It depends on how the evening goes," he replied. "Okay, Mr. Big Stuff. Have a good time," Kim said, smiling. "That's the plan. Well, I guess I'd better get dressed. See you later," Zayden commented as he closed her door and went to his room to get ready.

Zayden loved to dress to impress. After he showered and shaved, he put a little moose in his hair, then dressed in a nice pair of Zanella flat front fit slacks and a starched shirt he purchased weeks ago from Nordstrom before coming to Chicago. Whenever he traveled, Zayden was always prepared and packed for any occasion. He put on his favorite Armani cologne and was good to go. Zayden put on his matching dress jacket and took one last look in the mirror, checking to ensure he looked as handsome as he felt. You look good, boy, he said out loud as he turned to admire himself in several poses.

As Xander walked toward their bedroom to alert Kim that dinner was ready, he passed Zayden on his way out. "Man, you must have it bad for Danielle to get this dressed up for dinner," he said. Embarrassed at Xander's statement, Zayden stood tall and replied, "Bro, you know I don't do anything halfway. By the way, how do I look?" "You look very nice and have on some nice shoes, too," Xander commented, looking him up and down. "Yes, he does," Kim said, overhearing their conversation as she walked out of the room. Do I hear future wedding bells? She asked Zayden, and they burst out in laughter. "You two are funny, you know that?" Zayden said, still laughing. Anyway, my rideshare is here, and I can't have the lady waiting. I'll see you guys later, as he walked toward the door to leave.

Kim and Xander finished dinner and cleaned the kitchen together. He tried his best to get her back in bed, but lost the battle. With a break from his kitchen duties, Xander reviewed the advertisement that Kim had created. "This is good," he said, nodding his head. I will call the paper and place the ad when I get to the office tomorrow.

"Oh, I forgot to mention that I called Danielle back, and she is coming to visit tomorrow. She is taking the day off, so you don't have to worry. "I won't be alone," Kim said. "I don't worry," Xander said, smiling sheepishly. But I am glad she will be here with you. I'll only be gone for half of the day, so if you want, I can bring home some lunch. "That would be great!" Kim replied. I will let Danielle know when she gets here tomorrow, provided Zayden doesn't keep her out too late. She giggled. "Good, I'll call you before I leave work and see what you have a taste for, and we'll go from there," he said. Okay, thanks, she said. They showered and sat up in bed watching movies until falling asleep in each other's arms.

Chapter 18

After an exhausting afternoon of non-stop yoga and aerobic classes, Danielle was a little exhausted, but not too exhausted to see Zayden again. Everything that she enjoyed for breakfast was gone, and her stomach was starting to rumble from hunger. Zayden, on the other hand, was relaxed by now, she thought. He mentioned to Danielle that he was going straight back to his brother's house to take a long nap, so she was almost sure he would be well-rested for their date. Zayden explained to Danielle that he would choose the restaurant for the evening and chose Perry's Steakhouse & Grill. The two were to meet there at 7:00 p.m.

Zayden had a couple of days left to enjoy the Windy City, and Danielle wanted to leave a lasting impression. When she arrived home, Danielle grabbed a bottle of water and took a much-needed shower. After she got out of the shower, Danielle sat down and drank a protein drink so her stomach wouldn't be making growling and rumbling sounds at the dinner table. She had been daydreaming about this date all day long, and she wanted everything to be perfect. And now it's time to put the show on the road.

Danielle had chosen to wear a mini royal blue sequined dress with silver heels and a matching clutch purse. Before dressing, Danielle pinned up her braids and finished them off with a diamond-encrusted silver hair comb. She completed her makeup, and her face looked naturally flawless. As she finished dressing, she looked at herself in the floor mirror at different angles and determined that she looked good as she strutted toward her front door. It appears she and Zayden have the same idea of impressing one another. She grabbed her keys, set the house alarm, and walked out the door for the evening.

Zayden departed from his house early to get Danielle something special for their date. He didn't want to get anything overtly extravagant, but something delicate and charming to express his admiration for her. He had the driver take him to Helen Ficalora, near downtown Chicago. Zayden remembered Danielle wearing hoop earrings the night of Xander and Kim's dinner party and again when they had breakfast. He wanted to buy her something unique and completely off-the-cuff. Glancing to the left, his eyes caught a pair of 18k gold open circle dangle earrings with a Pave' diamond.

Being well-established and having a track record of achievements, he spares no expense in enhancing his lifestyle. So, it didn't take him long to choose the perfect gift. He had the jeweler wrap the red velvet box in gold wrapping paper with a small red bow. He placed it in his pocket, got back into the Uber, and proceeded to the restaurant. He was about fifteen minutes early, even after picking up flowers on the way there. Zayden had already included a tip when paying for the rideshare but tipped the driver again before getting out of the car. The driver was pleased and thanked Zayden profusely.

When he got out, he immediately spotted Danielle coming from the opposite direction. At a distance, he was stunned to see her beauty glow against the backdrop of the descending moonlight. His eyes danced from head to toe, admiring her as she strutted like a supermodel down a catwalk. Smiling, Zayden composed himself as she got closer. Immediately, they embraced, and he kissed her on the cheek as he handed her the bouquet of roses. "These are so pretty." You didn't have to do that, she said. "Pretty flowers for a sexy lady," he commented as he smiled from ear to ear. Zayden politely took her hand and placed it inside his arm, and they walked into the restaurant to the front counter. Zayden called in advance for the reservation, so there was no wait time.

The restaurant had a flare about it. There was a huge wine station on one side of the seating areas, a beautiful glass bar with gold inlay, and chandeliers with hanging crystals illuminating the entire room. There was architecturally sculpted lighting in other private areas of the restaurant that could be seen from a distance. "The ambiance here is beautiful, Zayden," Danielle commented as she looked around, surveying the restaurant. "Not as stunning and beautiful as you are in that dress," he replied. "This old thing?" Danielle said, smiling. Thank you very much, sir. "And what about you, looking debonair yourself?" Oh, I just pulled something out of the closet. Zayden lowered his head, smiling too. "Anyway, let's sit down and have some dinner, we are turning heads in here," he said, and they both laughed.

A waiter arrived with warm rolls, poured them glasses of water, and asked if they were ready to order. An appetizer was declined. Zayden ordered a bottle of Perry's Reserve Chardonnay. We will need a few minutes to look over the menu, he responded. The waiter nodded and said he would be back with the wine. Zayden leaned in and whispered to Danielle, "You look beautiful tonight." "Ditto," she said as she shyly smiled at him.

As they talked more about the design of the restaurant, the waiter returned with the wine and glasses. He popped the cork and poured wine into each of their glasses. He then placed the bottle in the gold ice bucket next to the table for easy access and indicated he would return for their orders. Zayden picked up his glass, raised it, and said, "Let's toast to a wonderful evening." Danielle obliged him by doing the same. They tapped the crystal glasses as they lingered, looking into each other's eyes, until they finally broke away to review the menu.

The waiter returned, and Danielle had noticed the vegan entrees, so she ordered the Vegan Skillet Chopped Steak served with a chargrilled vegetable trio, and Zayden ordered the Steakhouse Brick Chicken with Truffle Merlot Demiglace and a chargrilled vegetable trio. "I didn't realize you were vegan," Zayden said, looking confused. "Yes, most of the time. Lately, though, I've been slacking, but pretty much staying the course," Danielle replied. I've really been enjoying myself the last few weeks, with the wedding and everything, and with you too. Well, I hope I wasn't that much of a distraction, he shyly said. "No, I'm enjoying life," she said. After what happened to Kim and me, I've come to love myself and not sweat the small stuff like missing a vegan meal. Zayden felt for her, and his face said it all.

But you know what? I'll be okay. So, let's just enjoy the evening, okay? "Are you sure you're okay?" Zayden questioned. "Yes, I'm good," Danielle responded as she perked up.

Zayden thought for a moment that it was a good time to give Danielle the surprise gift, so he pulled it from his pocket and slid it on the table over to her. "What is this?" she questioned. Zayden said, "Hopefully, it's something that will put a smile back on that beautiful face of yours." Danielle unwrapped the package and opened the red velvet box. She put one hand on her open mouth when she saw the elegant earrings. She looked up at Zayden with tears in her eyes. He immediately rushed to her side, taking a handkerchief from his pocket to catch her tears. Danielle was at a loss for words. "Zayden, I don't know what to say," Danielle said, sniffing and surprised. "It's okay; you don't need to say anything. The light shown in your face is enough," he said. He wiped the tears from her eyes and kissed her on the cheek. Everything will be okay. "Thank you, I love them," she said in a crackling voice. "No thanks are needed," Zayden replied. You're worth it.

"I think I'll go to the powder room and freshen up this face of mine," Danielle said with a faint smile. Zayden watched her walk away and hoped his gift helped her feel better. While in the powder room, Danielle questioned herself. She looked into her teary eyes in the mirror and wondered if she was dreaming. All my adult life, I only had men who used and abused me. They never took the time to know who I was. Zayden is different from any man I have ever dated. Lord, am I worthy of this type of man, or is he another man who manipulates my feelings? Time will tell, she said to herself. She took out her makeup bag, touched up her face, and valiantly walked back to her seat.

When Danielle returned to the table, so did the waiter with their entrees. They indulged in friendly conversation while enjoying their meals. Everything was going well, and Danielle appeared happier to be with such a kind and thoughtful man. Zayden wanted to leave a lasting impression, and he did.

The night was right on track for a great evening. They even taste-tests each other's meals. Danielle laughed at the expression on Zayden's face as he placed vegan food in his mouth. "I think I'll watch my physique without the vegan and continue to work out," he smiled, and Danielle laughed hard. You need to come to my gym for a personal training session workout so I can see what cha' got, she said sarcastically. "Maybe I will when I come back to Chicago, which will be when the Carlisle baby comes, he replied. That little bundle is due a few months from now. "Okay, that's a deal!" Danielle said as she held back the sadness she felt of him leaving soon.

They had been in the restaurant for close to three hours when the waiter returned to confirm everything was going well and asked if they would be having dessert. Zayden requested the dessert menu. The waiter removed their plates as they reviewed the luscious desserts. Zayden looked at Danielle and asked if she would enjoy Bananas Foster. "Sure, that will be fine," she said. Good choice, the waiter replied.

Zayden then poured the two of them another glass of Chardonnay as the waiter left to complete their order. After the indulgence of their dessert, the evening was coming to an end. Danielle made a bold move and asked Zayden if he would like to come to her house for the night since it was getting late. "Sure, if it's not too much trouble," he said. "No, no trouble at all. I'm taking off tomorrow to visit with Kim most of the day, so we can go there together if that's okay with you," she asked. Danielle wanted more time with Zayden before he left Chicago. "Okay, um...let me give my brother a call and let him know that I won't be back tonight. I would not want him to worry about me if that's still a thing, Zayden replied as he laughed.

Zayden called Xander and paid the check. He helped Danielle with her shawl, and they left, walking to her car parked nearby. When they got to the car, he opened the door for her, turned, and their eyes met. Zayden gave Danielle a longing kiss before she stepped into the car. He walked to the passenger side, got in, and looked at her with sparks in his eyes. On the way to her condo, they laughed and talked about the good time they had at dinner and the good times they hope the future may bring them. Danielle soon pulled into her garage.

As soon as they walked through the door, Zayden was astounded by her condo's layout and the exquisite artwork. "I purchased some of the art from an estate sale. The owner passed away suddenly, and the executor of the estate sold everything at enormously cheap prices to empty the house as quickly as possible," she said. "It appears whoever the pieces belonged to had great taste," Zayden mused. "I thought they were great pieces myself," Danielle replied.

Danielle asked if he wanted something to drink. She mentioned having bottles of Michelob and water. I'll take a beer, he replied. Danielle pulled two beers from the fridge and gave one to Zayden as he admired the art. As she walked to the sofa, Danielle said, "I paid less than one hundred dollars for each piece. It almost felt like stealing. I thought I had hit the jackpot that day." "You did," Zayden said, laughing. "I did what?" Danielle said, squinting her eyes. "Won the jackpot," Zayden said, puzzled. "Oh, I thought you were saying I stole them," Danielle seriously said. Zayden burst out laughing, kissed her on the forehead, and held her tightly. His arms around her made her body tingle all over.

By the way, when will you be leaving? Danielle asked as they both sat down. "The day after tomorrow," Zayden replied. I'm sure I will have plenty of work waiting for me. "Isn't that always the case?" she asked. I realized Cooperate America was not for me years ago. That is why I started Core's Gym. It has always been a passion of mine to help individuals get fit and stay healthy. I love it. "I'm sure you're good at it too," Zayden commented. You'll see when you come back. I'm holding you to that personal training session, remember that. Okay, Danielle promised, holding up two fingers and making the peace sign. The two of them sat talking and listening to jazz as they had a second beer. They talked about past relationships and assured each other they had no significant others in their lives.

"I'm really going to miss you Zayden, Danielle said with sadness on her face. You have been such a delight to my spirit ever since I met you. The time we've spent together has been nothing short of amazing, and I thank you." This has been the best time I've had in a very long time. There were times when I didn't think I would ever be happy in my life again, but you changed all that for me. For that, I thank you from the bottom of my heart." Zayden responded, "It has been my pleasure. I feel the same way about you, too. It seems like the universe brought us together out of nowhere, and that is a good feeling."

As they looked into each other's eyes, Danielle leaned in, giving Zayden a kiss that was so intense that the two of them got lost in each other. When she slowly pulled away, they again looked at each other and then started to kiss passionately. Danielle stood up, grabbed him by the hand, and tugged his hand signaling for him to stand up. She hugged and kissed him one more time before leading him into her bedroom.

Once they entered the room, Danielle began to undress Zayden, and he followed her in earnest. At that moment, neither had a care in the world. The heat of the second kiss pulled them closer together. After they were completely unclothed, Zayden picked Danielle up and slowly laid her on the bed. He had reservations about what they were about to experience, and Danielle quietly assured him that she was okay with it. Zayden needed her as much as she needed him. She exhaled, lying there on her back, as Zayden began to pleasure her everywhere that he could so she would feel the comfort and connection of his body, soul, and mind. Her body begins to feel the urge for his body to take over. Zayden could feel her trembling, and he knew it was time for her to have all of him.

The foreplay began to fade into the climax that they both needed. Zayden looked at Danielle, and she looked at him with so much love in her eyes. He then slowly penetrated her, and she moaned lightly. As he stroked back and forth with ease, Danielle moaned with smiles of enjoyment, giving everything she had as she held tightly onto Zayden. They made love into the late-night hours until they fell asleep in each other's arms. Relaxing in a bed of passion, the couple consummated their long-distance love and respect for each other.

Chapter 19

Raven returned to her room and immediately grabbed her computer and paper to create a list of investigative services. She searched on Google for private investigators and their experience levels. Whoever she chose would need to be discreet, honest, and reliable. As she was reading, her phone rang. It was her brother, Harold.

"Hey Harold," she answered. How are you? "I'm fine," he replied. Sis, good news! You got a full price offer from a buyer today. It's a nice couple who are moving from New Jersey. To close the deal in 30 days, they want you to pay all closing costs. Since you had already anticipated this and the offer was for the full price, I went ahead and signed the offer on your behalf. The closing date has not been scheduled, so you will need to be here to complete everything because I will be traveling with my daughter and her family in a couple of days. We're going to Canada for a few weeks, and I don't want you to miss out on this.

"That is great news on both fronts," Raven commented. It's about time you get out of that house and start living life. I will make plans to be home in the next few days. Since I haven't seriously been looking for a smaller place, I'll need to hire a professional packing service and a moving company to transport everything to a storage facility.

"So, have you been having fun touring in Chicago?" Harold asked. I've heard the Navy Pier is a great place to visit. "Yes, I'm having a lot of fun and meeting such interesting people. I haven't visited the Navy Pier yet, but I plan to. Chicago has enormously tall buildings that you will practically break your neck trying to see to the top! And the architecture is simply breathtaking. Raven put on a good act for her brother so he wouldn't worry about her. "Well, I guess things are going well. I can sense it in your voice, Sis. I can't lie, though. I was worried about you for a while," Harold commented. "I know you were, but I am fine," Raven assured him. I plan to return once I close on the house. I want to see more outside of the city. Who knows? I may decide to move here one day. "You're kidding!" Harold said. He was taken aback by Raven's statement. You're not serious, are you? "Yes, I am serious, Raven affirmed.

Chicago is a big city with lots to see and do. I want to enjoy life as much as I can, Harold. I didn't get to do a lot of traveling when my husband was living because he was always traveling for work, and Eric, sadly, never invited me to come here. He always had an excuse. "So now it is my time to do as I please," she explained. "I guess I understand, just as long as you keep in touch with the family," Harold replied. Remember, we love you too. "I know that," Harold said. I love my family, but my nearest and dearest are no longer with me. I'm doing what makes me happy, okay? "Okay, Sis, I gotcha," he agreed.

Anyway, I hope everything goes as you expect it to. Be like me, Harold; you have to enjoy life to the fullest while you can. "And thank you once again, Harold, for handling the sale of my house on my behalf. I'll bring you something nice from Chicago," she said gratefully. "You don't have to do that, but okay" Harold laughed. I will talk with you later, Sis. "Okay, bye, boy," she said, smiling as she hung up the phone.

Raven continued her search for investigators that interested her within the Chicago area and that she felt would meet and execute her needs, so she started to make the calls. She explained what was needed, their discretion, and that if they completed everything requested, there would be a bonus. She took notes as they explained their services.

All of the investigators she spoke with seemed to understand the job, but she only needed one of them. So, to be fair, she told each of them she would call back when she made a final decision, and they understood. Looking into Kimberly Casey's life would require total discretion, given her outstanding reputation in the Chicago community. Raven kept thinking, so she needed the complete cooperation of whomever she chose. She carefully reviewed the notes taken from each investigator's interview. She would want to meet with them in their office and would pay whatever it took to get what she needed. Fast-forwarding her decision on this venture was of the essence before she left to go home in the next week.

For many hours, Raven went back and forth, scrutinizing the reviews of the investigators. After much thought, Raven decided to go with Prime Investigative Services. She would contact them early in the morning. Raven also decided to check out of the hotel the day she leaves for home and return to a rental place until her task is completed. There was lots to do, and she had very little time to put her plot in place. Raven decided to shower and get a good night's sleep before moving full steam ahead to get all the preparation behind her.

When she woke up the next day, Raven made herself a cup of coffee from the coffee bar, ordered a full breakfast, read the paper, and listened to the news in the background. When she finished, she called Prime Investigators to schedule an appointment to speak with an investigator that same day. Simultaneously, she searched for a house rental so that when she returned to Chicago, she would be set up to move into her new home.

Raven located several expensive homes with rental prices up to $6000 per month. She reviewed photos of gated communities with huge master bedrooms and baths, high-quality chef's kitchens with islands, parlors, game rooms, breakfast and dining rooms, huge garages, and cameras inside and out, as well as surveillance and security cameras for the entire community. She made calls to view a few after leaving the investigator's office. It was going to be a busy day for Raven, but she thought it would be all worth it.

Raven got ready, called for a ride-share, and left for the investigator's office. Raven arrived and entered the 54-story gold-glazed glass building with double doors. As she entered the elevator, the warm, relaxing colors and classical music lifted her spirits as the doors smoothly opened on the 35th floor. She walked to the front desk, gave her name, and Tim Connors was called. Looking around, Raven admired the uniqueness and richness of the lobby. Her impression of the area soon dissipated as Tim came out and introduced himself. Raven stood up and they shook hands. Tim then walked her down a long hallway with a dark blue carpet coupled with a colorful oriental design tufted on both sides. He led her straight to his office and offered her something to drink, and Raven accepted a bottle of water.

When they settled in, Tim explained his services and the retainer. She nodded and agreed with his proposal. He then proceeded to ask Raven what he could do for her. She pulled out photos of Kimberly Casey and Danielle Moore. She made it very clear that she wanted a thorough background investigation on the two of them— anything he could find, the good and the bad. To sweeten the deal, Raven reiterated that there would be a bonus for exceptional work. Tim understood. Raven firmly repeated, "I mean everything you can find." She pulled out cash for the retainer and handed it over to Mr. Connors. To not draw suspicion, Raven chose not to write a check that revealed her married name and instead continued using her maiden name to conceal her true identity.

"Ms. Wilder, I will give you my utmost expertise and do my absolute best" to get the information you want. "Remember, this is to be discreet, and most of all, confidential," she said. "I understand and will get on it right away," Tim responded. I will make every effort to get back to you as quickly as possible. "Thank you," Raven replied. Raven got up from her seat, as did Tim, and she said with a piercing look, "I hope to hear back from you soon, Mr. Connors." Walking back through the lobby with fire in her eyes, Raven was determined to destroy the people who were responsible for her son's demise. "I will see you soon, Ms. Wilder," he said. Raven nodded and got on the elevator. Her ride-share was waiting to transport her to the home of Frank Jennings, the builder of the community and homeowner of a home she wanted to check out.

Mr. Jennings was outside the door, awaiting Raven's arrival. He introduced himself, and they exchanged pleasantries. He opened the door for her to walk in. The ride-share waited for her once again. Raven looked up at the high ceilings she saw in the search photos, and they were more elegant than she thought. Frank gave her a complete tour of the home, and she was in awe of everything she saw. The home was being rented with all furnishings. Afterward, Frank asked, "What do you think, Ms. Harris?" Does this home meet your needs? "Mr. Jennings, I must say, you did not miss a thing when building this home.

Have you ever lived here?" she asked. "Yes, I have. My wife, daughter, and I resided here until she went to college. My wife and I decided we wanted to be closer to her for anything that she might need. "And yes, to answer that questionable look, we are doting parents." We bought a small house near the campus, and we'll be there for about another year, just until she graduates. That's why we are only renting the house for six months if that will be enough time for you. "Oh yes, that will be more than enough, and it is certainly big enough," Raven excitedly said.

"Will someone be in the home with you?" Jennings asked. "No, it will be just myself," Raven answered. I have business in Chicago that will take an ample amount of time, and this would be perfect. When would be a good time to move in?" she asked. "Anytime would suffice. I will be leaving at the end of the week to go to Florida," Jennings explained. The rent will be $3300.00 a month, with the security deposit in the same amount. The deposit will be refunded, provided the home remains in the same condition as rented. "I understand, Mr. Jennings," she replied.

I have the papers right here if you would like to complete a rental application. Yes, sir," she said as he pulled out a chair for her. After conducting a credit check, if it is approved, I will provide you with the keys. "Great," Raven eagerly said as she completed the application. Raven handed Frank Jennings the application and thanked him for the house tour. Frank nodded and said it shouldn't take more than a day or so to get the report, and I will contact you as soon as I get it. Raven politely said that once she heard from him, she would bring cash for the rent and deposit. He and Raven shook hands, and he walked her to the door. Raven decided she didn't need to look any further, so she called and canceled the appointments on her way back to the hotel. It had been a long day for Raven, and all she wanted to do now was have dinner and sleep.

When Raven got back to the hotel, she gave her driver a hefty tip for his patience throughout the day. She then went to the hotel restaurant for dinner and noticed her favorite bartender, Jeff, was on duty. He came over to her and asked how she was doing. "It was a very productive day," Raven replied, nodding her head and raising her eyebrows with confidence. I haven't eaten since this morning, and now I'm famished. "Well, we need to get you some food, don't we?" he said, smiling. Jeff took her order, and she quietly nursed a glass of wine until her dinner of a steak, a baked potato, and a small salad arrived.

As Raven was unwrapping her napkin, Jeff walked over to her table and said, "You look different this evening." Smiling, Raven replied, "At last, it seems like everything is falling into place." "That's great; sometimes you have to be patient for the tide to turn in your favor," he said. "You're right," she said. This calls for a celebration and a glass of wine on me. Jeff went to the bar, got a bottle of wine, and refilled her glass. He turned around and skipped back to the bar. Raven was smiling and grinning from ear to ear.

Jeff was pleased to witness Raven's smile and laughter. He would periodically pass by her table and have a short conversation to keep her in an upbeat mood. The last time he passed by, she said goodnight, and he nodded with a smile as he delivered some drinks to his patrons. Raven left and went straight to her room, took a shower, put on her nightgown, and snuggled tightly into her down comforter.

Chapter 20

The sound of chirping birds outside her bedroom window woke Zayden and Danielle from a deep, restful sleep. Danielle rubbed her eyes and turned toward Zayden as they looked face-to-face into each other's eyes and smiled. With concern, Zayden asked, "Are you okay?" "Yeah, I'm more than okay, except...you are about to leave," Danielle replied with eyes of sadness. "Will I see you again?" she asked, propping her head up on her pillow. "Of course, you will. You are stuck with me," he commented with a smile. Exhaling slowly, Danielle murmured, "Good." I know we will be miles apart, and I've heard that long-distance relationships are hard to maintain and eventually fizzle out. "But we won't let that happen," Zayden assured. Danielle gave a thumbs up in agreement and smiled.

Last night was wonderful, she said. "I hope so, because I enjoyed you too," he answered. "Time sure does pass fast when you finally find your soulmate," Danielle said solemnly. We can spend the remainder of the day with my new sister since I am departing early tomorrow morning. "You're right! She added affirmatively. I'm taking off to spend time with Kim today and with you too." As the saying goes, "Two for the price of one!" It just doesn't get any better than that. I have a best friend, and I now have a new best friend.

Kim is not going to believe what happened between us. "I believe the two of them already know, especially after I didn't come home last night," Zayden said, laughing. Unquestionably, they will not believe that I slept outside in a tent somewhere, he said. They were still laughing. "Yeah, you might be right," Danielle replied. Let's prepare ourselves for a line of questioning, she said, half-jokingly. "I don't know... Xan is more of a laid-back type of guy. Oh, don't get me wrong; he'll joke about it, but it won't be anything that'll make us feel guilty. Besides, I believe they'll both be glad for us." "I guess you're right," Danielle commented. I'm going to take a shower; would you like to join me?" she asked seductively. "Don't mind if I do, milady," he replied.

After lovemaking in a long, warm shower, Danielle and Zayden got dressed. While he finished putting on his clothes, Danielle went into the kitchen, brewed the coffee, and warmed a variety of croissants in the oven. As Danielle cut up fresh fruit into bite-size pieces, Zayden asked if he could help her, which surprised her. She politely replied, "I've got it," but thank you. Danielle placed everything on a tray and put it on the dining room table, along with a place setting for two. She appeared to be happier than she'd ever been, and it showed in her face. The two seemed to be more than comfortable with each other now that they had consummated their love. Zayden promised to call her often, and Danielle promised the same. A branch of the technology company he worked for was located in Chicago, and Zayden thought that if everything continued to go well with him and Danielle, he might consider a transfer, although he didn't mention this to her. He wanted to be sure before saying anything.

After everything was cleaned up, Danielle and Zayden left to go to his brother's house. It was around 9:30 a. m. When they got there, Kim was up and dressed, stretched out on the sofa in the family room, watching her favorite childhood cartoon, The Jetsons. Xander had already left the house earlier to get to the office. The doorbell rang. Kim viewed the camera and saw Danielle and Zayden at the door. She got up from the sofa faster than she had in weeks to open the door. "Good morning, you two," Kim said. Come in. They all hugged. How was your evening? she asked. They answered in unison, Great! Kim led them to the family room and mentioned that Xander had already left. And, oh, before I forget, he will be back around 1 p.m. and bringing lunch. He said he would call to see what we all wanted before he left the office. So, have a seat. Zayden said, "I'm going to change clothes first, but I'll be back."

Danielle hugged her friend again and sat down. "Soooo, how are you feeling?" Danielle asked. "Believe it or not, I am doing a lot better." I'm at the end of the first trimester, and we are hoping for joy from now on. "I'll bet; I've heard how rough it can be," Danielle commented. Yeah, so what is it you wanted to talk to me about? Kim questioned. "It's a moot point now. I got my answer," Danielle replied. "Really?"... huh... okay," Kim commented.

Now answer my question, "How was your night?" she asked, smiling and looking directly into Danielle's eyes. Danielle couldn't hide her excitement and practically yelled it out and said with a low voice, "I had the time of my life!" It was a great night! Danielle shared everything but did not discuss their private moments. She did share enough so that Kim would get an idea of why she was so happy, though. "I am happy for you," Kim whispered. By that time, Zayden had walked into the room.

"What are you guys whispering about, as if I didn't know?" he asked, smiling. "We were catching up, girl stuff, you know," Kim replied. "Yeah, girl stuff." Danielle turned toward him, winking one eye with a smile. Zayden commented, "Right...Anyway, how are you doing, Sis? Is everything good with my little niece or nephew?" "Yes, Uncle Zayden, we are both doing fine," Kim smiled. I heard last night you guys had dinner at Perry's Steakhouse & Grill. Xander and I have eaten there many times, and the food was great. I understand you were not fond of Danielle's vegan entrée. Not so much, it's an acquired taste.

"So, when will the construction begin on Little Carlisle's room?" Zayden asked. "On Monday afternoon," Kim said. I'm not looking forward to all the noise, though, but there is no other way. It shouldn't take long. The contractor gave us an estimated time of 30 days since the room was already constructed when we built the house. When they complete it, I will start to decorate it with my designs. That's where you come in, Ms. Danielle. I am going to need your help. "Not a problem," Danielle said. "I'm just a phone call away." Danielle was grateful Kim allowed her to be in her life, and now she wanted her to be a part of her baby's life too, and her smiles said it all.

Zayden, "I know you'll be back after the birth, right?" Kim asked. "You know I will, Sis," he answered, sneaking a smile at Danielle. To see my big brother as a father will be a-ma-zing. When I called my parents to make sure they got home alright, Pops said that my mom had already started online baby shopping for the little tike. As for me, I'm just writing a check! Zayden said, laughing. Shopping takes way too much time, and writing a check only takes a minute. They all burst out laughing.

Kim's phone rang. It was Xander calling. "Hey baby," Kim voiced. "Hey yourself, how are you feeling?" he asked. "Great! Zayden and Danielle are here, keeping me in stitches. Good, he said. "So, what would you guys like to have for lunch?" "Hold for a minute," she said. Guys, Xander wants to know what you want for lunch. "Nothing in particular for me; how about you, Danielle? Zayden asked. Me too; I'm not choosy, Danielle replied. "Honey, no one is being picky. Whatever you decide will be fine," Kim said. "Okay, not a problem. See you guys later," Xander replied.

Xander arrived with jerk chicken, mashed potatoes, peas, rolls, and peach cobbler, which he had previously sampled at a nearby restaurant. Kim made a pitcher of iced tea, and everyone chowed down. They laughed and talked and were pleased with all the food, especially the homemade peach cobbler. During the conversation, Xander confirmed with Kim that he had placed the ad for a housekeeper. Zayden jokingly said, "Why did you do that? I could clean for you." There was silence in the room, then everyone looked at Zayden and burst out laughing.

"Boy, you couldn't even clean your bedroom when we were young. For us to be able to go anywhere, I had to help you, so dad wouldn't pull out his belt." So, no, that's okay, we'll go with a professional, Xander laughingly said. Zayden pretended to exhale in disappointment, and they continued their lunch, joking the entire time about their boyhood. Kim sat with her arms on the table and her hands under her chin, looking around at her family with so much admiration. She thought to herself how nice it was to see everyone happy and enjoying their time together. She again caught Zayden and Danielle with their eyes glued to each other from time to time.

After lunch, they were stuffed. Xander pulled out a couple of movies for everyone to decide. They all agreed to watch the Rocky movies, 1 through 4. It was late into the evening before they were all finished. No one was hungry, so Xander suggested a game of Monopoly. After a while, Kim decided she would lie down to rest. She and Danielle retreated to her bedroom and talked while Xander popped a bottle of champagne for himself and Zayden as they continued the game. Kim and Danielle continued their conversation about Danielle's evening with Zayden, and she was pleased to see her friend so happy. Kim began to feel sleepy after about an hour, so Danielle covered her with a blanket and tiptoed out of the room. She let Xander know that she was asleep, and he got up and went to check on her.

Zayden and Danielle sneaked a few kisses, went to the family room, and sat on the sofa. "I'm going to miss you when you leave in the morning," Danielle said. I will miss you more, Zayden said. "If I send you plane tickets, will you come up a few weekends?" he asked her. "Nothing can stop me," she said, smiling as tears welled up. "We're going to make this work, okay?" he said. "Okay," Danielle replied as a tear fell from one eye. "Baby, I'm not going anywhere." Just be patient with me. We will be fine, Zayden assured her. It's in the stars for us; I believe that, and I hope you believe it too. "I do," Danielle whispered in his ear. Zayden then leaned in and kissed her passionately.

Chapter 21

Raven gets to her hometown. and her stop is to see her brother, Harold. She didn't call, but to her surprise, he was home. He told her that his daughter, Kathy, and her family would be picking him up in the morning, and he was in the process of doing some last-minute packing. They talked about her trip to Chicago and her son's estate. Raven was vague and gave very little information on most of what occurred regarding Eric, nor did she expose what she was doing other than sightseeing and shopping.

Harold was unaware of her probe into the people Eric had personally interacted with or the money she had accumulated in his name. He glanced at her, realizing that the expensive clothes she had on indicated that it must be a considerable amount. He hadn't seen her so eloquently dressed since the day of her marriage many years ago and was eager to find out more.

"What's going on, Sis?" Harold asked. "What do you mean?" Raven replied, staring at him. "Well, for one thing, it's been ages since I've seen you dressed like this in the afternoon. It's around 1 o'clock, and you are dressed for an evening out," he commented. "I just wanted to dress comfortably after the long drive from Chicago," she said. "Ah.... most people driving long distances usually dress in something a little more comfortable, like jeans, t-shirts, or a warm-up and sneakers." Harold surmised. I-am-comfortable Harold, she said. I told you that I was doing what makes me feel good and happy, and that's what I'm doing.

Harold felt as though there was more to the story, but he didn't press the issue. He was glad she was in good spirits, and for now, that's all that mattered. Harold was still skeptical and wary. "I'm about to fix me some lunch. Do you have time to sit down with me?" he asked. "Sure, I came here first when I got back, so I haven't gone by the house yet," Raven said. "Don't worry, it's still intact," he said, smiling. Harold put together a couple of roast beef sandwiches, potato salad, and iced tea. Of course, this was nothing compared to the impeccable lifestyle and lavish spending of Eric's money in Chicago. They took a seat at his kitchen table and talked more about the places she had visited, including her exercising at the gym and her intention of returning to Chicago. "Why would you want to go back to that place, since you know... ?" Harold asked. He stopped short of mentioning Eric's name. "What's wrong with me going back!? You don't trust me to be alone? I can do that here! What do you think I'm going to do—fall apart!? Trust me, I will be fine!" Raven spat.

Apologetically, Harold looked at her in surprise. "I didn't mean to upset you; I was just wondering, that's all," he said. Raven exhaled with a huge sigh of relief." "No, I'm sorry. I guess I'm just tired from the drive," Raven said, covering up her antics. She couldn't let on that it was anything more than that. He would think she was crazy for attempting to clear her son's name, and maybe she was, even though Eric was guilty of his crimes. She was doing what she thought any mother would do. Anyway, like I mentioned to you a few days ago, I've had thoughts of moving there. Harold, I truly love the atmosphere; it takes me away from the grief of my son and gives me more things to think about and many things to do and enjoy. "I understand... And I'm glad you're happy," he said. If moving to Chicago is what you want to do, I'm behind you.

Kathy and the kids asked about you all the time and wondered when you would be back. "They miss you, Sis," Harold said. I miss them too, Harold," Raven said. "When and if I decide to move, I promise to spend more time with them before I do so," Raven sadly said. This is not something she thought about when she was thinking of moving away. She was so consumed with finding out more about Eric's personal life that she never thought about the rest of her family.

After lunch, they sat and talked for a few hours more. Harold filled her in more regarding the buyer of her house and suggested that she may want to contact their realtor. "I'll take care of that tomorrow," she replied. Raven decided it was finally time for her to get home and rest awhile. In the meantime, I need to prepare to move out. "Sorry, I won't be home to help you. You know you can stay here if you don't find anything temporary after the closing," Harold offered. "I may take you up on that," Raven said.

Anyway, I'd better get going before I pass out. And you, my brother, have a great time with the family. She kissed her brother on the cheek, and they hugged before he walked her to the door to leave. "You take care of yourself, Harold," she said. "I will, and you take care of yourself too, Sis," he replied.

As Raven pulled into her driveway, she noticed Harold had done a great job keeping up her yard and flowers while she had been away. She pushed the remote to open the garage, drove in, and walked into the house with her luggage. Considering the way she had lived it up for weeks, she almost felt like a peasant entering her ranch-style home. Eventually, reality set in, and she began to feel differently about her past lifestyle. One different thing is that she can now purchase or acquire anything her heart desires. Raven almost gave herself away with the outfit she wore home. Thankfully, Harold didn't continue to ask questions. She needed to be more subtle at home if she didn't want to look suspicious.

Exhausted, Raven took a shower, got a bottle of water from the refrigerator, and sat on the living room sofa with her head tilted back, listening to the sound of a Western TV program. She fell asleep and was later startled by the sound of gunshots on the show. Using the TV remote, Raven turned off the TV, dragged herself to the bedroom, and got into bed for the rest of the night.

Raven got up around 10 a.m., and went to the kitchen for coffee. There wasn't much in the fridge. Harold knew she would be on her way home soon, so he made sure bread, sausage, eggs, and juice were there for her. While cooking, Raven realized this was different from the room service she had become accustomed to and smiled to herself. She even reminisced about Jeff, the bartender, who provided support and comfort during her most challenging moments, bringing her food, drinks, and good conversation. Her racing mind went from life in Chicago, to a revenge plot against Eric's enemies and the sale of her house. She aimed to complete the house by separating storage items from the few items she intended to carry to Chicago. As well as awaiting a report from the investigator she hired.

After a satisfying breakfast and a thorough cleaning of the kitchen, she created a to-do list. First on the list is to call the realtor. Raven reached into her expensive purse and pulled out a Cassandre Matelassé business card case. She rambled through the holder until she found the realtor card. She called the buyer's realtor agent and introduced herself as the owner of the home. The realtor stated that if all goes well with the financing, the closing will occur within the next three to four weeks. Also, when the closing attorney receives and reviews all pertinent information, he will inform you of a possible closing date and time.

Raven politely thanked her, hung up and started searching for a storage facility and a professional packing and moving company. Knowing there wasn't much time, Raven began to make a mental note of items that needed to go into storage. Simultaneously, she is incoherent, muttering something about them telling lies, how they treated her son unfairly, and how it's almost time for vengeance.

Chapter 22

It's been weeks, and little Carlisle's room is coming together. Using her design, Kim hired a renowned artist to paint a colorful mural on the ceiling. She also purchased a custom crib, changing table, dresser, bookshelf, and other items that would make the room complete. Despite making only suggestions on the baby's room design, Xander is actively involved in supporting Kim by attending doctor's appointments and obtaining a housekeeper.

The interview of several housekeepers, which had been conducted out of more than fifty submitted applications, had finally come to an end with three applicants meeting their criteria and expectations. Xander employed and submitted the application and references of Isabel Iglesias to Truth Finder, a reliable background service. She is their first choice, whom they both felt was more personal and the most qualified of the applicants. Within days, Truth Finder returned a thorough background and criminal report. After reviewing the report, Xander and Kim comfortably made their decision to hire Isabel Iglesias. Her references from previous clients were impeccable in every sense of the word.

Isabel Iglesias was so grateful for the opportunity to work for Kim and Xander. Shortly after, she soon moved into the maid's private living quarters within the house. After Isabel finished unpacking, she sat down with Kim and Xander in the dining room to discuss her salary and her household responsibilities. Isabel understood and was ready to get started. Excitedly, she said, "I need to start dinner." They all smiled. Before laying down for a nap, Kim gave her a tour of the kitchen. It didn't take long before Isabel indoctrinated herself into their kitchen routines.

Within hours, she had the table set and the food ready to be served. Isabel was so excited about the dishes that she had chosen to put on the table. When Kim and Xander entered the room, they were blown away. Affectionally, Isabel had used Kim's quilted design with a silver-rimmed place setting that she had forgotten existed. Kim asked Xander to go and get her phone. When he returned, she took a picture of the table and sent it to Danielle. They were the dishes that Danielle had purchased for her at an estate sale. Isabel, who is of Cuban descent, is skilled at cooking traditional Cuban food as well as American cuisine.

Great strides were made to complete the nursery in record time before Kim's delivery date. The construction work is complete, and now the artist is painting Kim's mural design on the ceiling. Even though everything was on track, Kim was bored out of her mind and begged Xander to allow her to take on small projects that she could complete in her home studio. She promised to sit on the couch with her desk and take mini breaks to prop up her feet and rest. He couldn't deny Kim anything whenever she gave him the infamous sheepish grin.

Agreeing with her sentiment, he suggested that the projects be no larger than 20 x 17 in size, and he reminded her to Zoom her clients. When and if the clients were to pick up their projects, Isabel was instructed to be by her side at all times. That was his requirement. Importantly, Xander wanted her to open the window and use the circulating fan to move the paint fume away from her. Kim wobbled over to Xander to give him a thank-you and a hug. Simultaneously, they burst out laughing at the sight of Kim trying to center her belly to keep from losing her balance.

After weeks of planning and designing, Kim was very pleased with the nursery results. With the assistance of Isabel and Danielle, who were more than grateful to help, everything started to fall into place. Isabel dusted the furniture and vacuumed the newly laid carpet, and Danielle hung most of the small artwork and placed baby items on the bookshelf. We are lucky to have chosen Isabel as our housekeeper. She is a hard worker, respectful, and loyal to the family. To show our appreciation, Isabel was given the option of a salary with a bonus or a salary with quality time with her family, but not a long vacation at this time due to Kim's due date.

Isabel plays a crucial role in keeping the house organized, cooking, and also helping Kim with her necessities when needed. She is not only their housekeeper but has become an integral part of their family unit. (Danielle, a family friend, assists when needed.) Danielle and Xander hung the bigger art pieces and moved the baby furniture into its designated areas. The baby's room was almost as large as their master bedroom and is now decorated from ceiling to floor. Given the abundance of gifts already received, it is obvious the grandparents will thoroughly adore and spoil the Carlisle addition.

Kim, nearing the end of her pregnancy, was recently reintroduced to a diet high in nutrients and low in sugar, salt, and fats. For that reason, Isabel was asked to prepare separate meals for the two of them. Without wavering, Isabel agreed and prepared a grocery list from the booklet Kim received from her doctor. Kim informed Isabel that Danielle would be staying with her tomorrow while she was shopping.

While Isabel went grocery shopping, Danielle stayed with Kim for a few hours so that she wouldn't be home alone. "You know, Danielle, Isabel is a jewel," Kim said. "I am so happy for you guys," Danielle replied. Are you doing everything the doctor told you to do? "How can I not? Xander has Isabel on daily patrol. Eating schedule. Vitamin regimen. Nap time. What more can a girl ask for?" Kim told her as they laughed out loud.

Yes, I am doing everything I've been told, and I feel good. I'm just sitting back, awaiting this little sweetheart as she rubs her stomach. Oh, by the way, Xander cleared me to do some small art projects in the studio, but not without restrictions. I called Monica to let her know, and she agreed to bring me some supplies since I have very little here to work with. She was reluctant at first, but Xander put her mind at ease. He also made sure to tell her what size canvases to bring. Xander doesn't want me to stress over anything. She is just as protective as he is, more or less, but I do understand her concerns.

"To be honest, Kim, so am I," Danielle replied, but if Xander is okay with it, then I am too. I can go by your office and pick up everything to save Monica a trip if you want me to. "That would be great!" Kim is filled with immense excitement. I will call Monica and ask her to pack everything so you can pick them up as soon as possible. "You are really excited about this, huh?" Danielle asked. "Yes, sitting around being bored is not my strong suit, and it is wearing me out," Kim commented. Isabel will not allow me to even pick up a glass, and Xander, well, he is just as bad. "When the baby is born, it will give the two of them something else to focus on," Kim replied. Besides, I just thought about it; we will all be busy, and they both laughed.

Isabel returned, and Danielle stayed a while longer. Kim called Monica and explained to her that Danielle would be picking up the supplies in the next day or two. She reiterated everything that she needed to complete various projects. Monica understood and would have the supplies ready for pick-up. Monica also stated that she and Jay would be out to see them sometime in the next week.

Kim said she is looking forward to seeing them. They said their goodbyes and hung up.

It was time for Danielle to leave, so Kim stood up, and the two hugged as Xander walked in the door. "Hi Danielle," he said as she was leaving. "Hi yourself, and take care of my girl," she said as she waved and got into her car to leave.

"Hey, babe, how was your day? Not too strenuous, I hope," Xander jokingly asked. "It was good; the police patrol was all over it today," Kim laughed. She continued to talk about her day with Danielle. She agreed to pick up the supplies and bring them to me in a couple of days. "That's good," but remember, Kim, do not work hard at any of this," he commented. "I won't, sweetheart, just baby steps," she replied, and Xander smiled at her.

Chapter 23

Zayden was sitting in his office, thinking about the last time he and Danielle spent together. It had been months since they were together in the same room. They have shared conversations via Zoom and also talked on the phone, but today would be different. She was coming to visit for the first time and was due to arrive soon. Zayden looked at his hands and noticed his palms sweating. Nervousness was reeling all over him, and he didn't know why. Other than that, he was glad she was coming.

For months, he had thought of this day, and now the time has come. Zayden had a professional cleaning service detail his townhome from top to bottom for Danielle's weekend stay. He bought new linens for each of the bedrooms and new towel sets for the bathrooms. Zayden planned to cook for her during the short visit so he stocked his fridge with foods appealing to her. He also placed fresh flowers on the dining room table, reflecting on Xander giving Kim flowers and saying to himself, Big brother, you taught me well.

Zayden cleared his desk and finished up all the last-minute details before heading out to the airport. He made arrangements to leave early to pick up Danielle so that he wouldn't run into traffic. It was Friday, and traffic was always at its worst. Finally, he made it to the airport terminal, where he purchased flowers for her as a welcoming gift. After all the rushing, he realized he was earlier than he had anticipated. Looking at his hands, they were sweating again, and his legs began to feel heavy.

Zayden decided to sit down at one of the restaurants on sight near the gate to have a glass of sweet iced tea. While sipping the tea, he thought of the fun the two of them would have during Danielle's visit. He missed her so much and intended to show her how much when she got there. The sound of the speaker announcing Danielle's flight number interrupted his thoughts. The plane had arrived and was approaching the gate. Zayden took a deep breath and exhaled.

Nervously, he walked to the gate, drying his hands with the napkins that he had picked up at the restaurant. Danielle appeared in straight-leg jeans, a turtleneck sweater, a jacket, and the cute polar fleece hat and gloves set Zayden sent her weeks ago for the trip. As she looked around for him, their eyes met. Their smiles were as large as the moon. As they approached one another, it seemed as though they were walking in slow motion. They came closer until their lips met, and kisses were planted as the fireworks went off in their heads.

Afterward, Zayden grabbed her bag and took her by the hand, and they strolled to the car like two teenagers on their first date. "I am so glad to see you," he said, breaking the silence. I cannot believe you are here. We've finally synced our schedules, and you're here! "Zayden, I've missed you so much, and I'm so happy you invited me. And thank you again for the hat and glove set. I love them," Danielle excitedly replied. "You're very welcome. I told you that I would. I always try to keep my word, at least most of the time, and he smiled. Jokingly, Danielle mimicked a legendary TV commercial, "I like a man who keeps his word." They laughed so hard and loudly that people stopped to see what was so funny.

Feeling embarrassed, they rushed to Zayden's car, got in, and sealed their first joke together with an intimate kiss. "So, what should we do first?" he asked. "Well, I am just a tad bit famished," she said. "Somehow, I knew you would be, so I'm taking you to this little bistro spot I know you will enjoy," he commented. And they serve vegans! "You didn't have to do that. This weekend I am going all out and enjoying the finer things in life," Danielle laughed. "In that case, how about some cheeseburgers and fries?" Zayden asked. "Sounds good. Don't mind if I do," she said. Zayden drove to a little burger spot called Burger & Things, a quaint little restaurant similar to Burger King but with a more elaborate menu. The two enjoyed cheeseburgers, seasoned fries, and real vanilla milkshakes while talking about Zayden's future niece or nephew, Kim, Xander, their new housekeeper, and work. They sat there for a few hours longer before leaving for Zayden's townhouse.

He drove through the gates of his townhome community. Danielle looked surprised because it appeared to be nothing like she expected. The community was of the highest caliber and gave off the impression that it was only for the most elite people. Zayden parked the car, got out, and graciously helped Danielle to her feet. As she walked through the foyer into the main living area, she was astounded by the room's expansiveness, which included floor-to-ceiling windows and a cathedral ceiling. Her eyes were mesmerized as she admired the grayish-blue, custom-flowing drapes.

While still in her dreamlike state, Zayden put her bag down, removed the backpack from her shoulders, and gave her an affectionate hug. In a gentle tone, Zayden asked, "Would you like a tour?" "Of course," she said with a big smile. He picked up her bag and dropped it off in his bedroom, then proceeded to give her a tour of his home, which was three stories. The expression on Danielle's face was priceless, and Zayden shook his head, smiling at her. "Your home is absolutely fabulous!" she said excitedly. I never thought it would be this large inside, viewing it from the outside." "It surprised me too when I toured the model," he commented. I love it. It's more than enough space for me.

My parents thought it was a little too much space. They said I wouldn't be able to keep it clean, given how I kept my room at home when Xan and I were young. I must admit, though, that I did have it professionally decorated. I also had a cleaning lady come in and touch it up before your arrival. Since dusting is not my thing, the cleaning lady comes in periodically and handles that kind of stuff. I used to watch my mom go from one room to another with furniture polish and dusting materials. That is not me. Now, I will take out the trash all day before you put me in an apron and cleaning attire. The laughter was so intense that tears fell from their eyes when he said that. As a guy, other than dusting, I keep a pretty decent standard of cleanliness. Other than that, simultaneously shrugging his shoulders, I keep it pretty decent.

"Well, I must say, it is one of the finest townhomes I've seen in a while," Danielle said. I knew that I had a nice one myself, but it doesn't compare to yours at all. "Oh, don't downplay yourself, Zayden said. These homes were built just over a year ago. And over time, as you may know, things change from year to year in most areas.

The newer architects are always evolving by creating or designing something more glamorous, unique, and practical to obtain the best in their particular area of expertise. I understand, and your home is just as nice. The style is exquisite, the décor is classy and timeless, and it is also a perfect reflection of your personality. Danielle smiled, leaning her head to the side. I imagine that if I resided in Chicago, I'm sure I would have something similar.

Anyway, enough of that. You're here to have fun. So, go freshen up, and I'll pop a bottle of wine, create a charcuterie board, and we can relax to some music." "That sounds good; I think I will," Danielle replied. "I've put your bag in my room if you're comfortable with that," he said. "Yes, that's fine," she said, walking up the stairs. You'll find everything you need in the bathroom, he hollered to her. Okay! She hollered back.

When Danielle returned, Zayden had everything laid out perfectly, and the charcuterie board was fit for a queen. The board was laid out with two types of meat, various cheeses, fruit, and crackers, with small plates, forks, and linen napkins on the side. She was overwhelmed, and Zayden didn't notice the look of surprise on her face. He had already filled the wine glasses with white wine and had them in his hand as he walked to her, kissed her on the cheek, and handed her a glass. Lit candles were scattered throughout the room, while the background was filled with soothing jazz music.

This is all very nice, Zayden," she said. "It's all for you, sweetheart," he replied. They sat down, and he gave her a napkin, a plate and a fork. Danielle put her glass down on the gold-encrusted coaster, filled her small plate with some of the meats, some cheese, a few pieces of fruit, and a couple of the crackers, and sat back on the sofa. She then said, smiling, "I don't know what to say other than you went all out, Mister." I appreciate the hospitality so far. "You are welcome. I do what I can," he said jokingly. He told her to get as comfortable as she liked.

"Put your feet up," he told her. "On your sofa?" she questionably asked. "Sure, not a problem," Zayden replied. Danielle removed her sneakers and pushed herself to the back of the sofa for comfort. "Now, doesn't that feel better?" he asked. "Yes, it does; thank you," she said. Zayden got up and excused himself to change out of his monkey suit, which is what he called his suit and tie, in the middle of their conversation and returned minutes later to get comfortable as well.

The two of them stretched out on the sofa and enjoyed themselves talking, laughing, and listening to jazz well into the late-night hours. They finished the entire bottle of wine, consumed most of the items on the board, and soon realized the time had quickly passed. Zayden cleared and cleaned up everything on the table. Danielle assisted him. Afterward, they went upstairs to bed.

Danielle was feeling tipsy, and she suggested they shower together before bed. Zayden smiled at her and was all too happy to oblige. The exhilarating sensation of the water spraying from the showerhead warmed their bodies to the point where the two began to feel the sexual heat within themselves. When getting out of the shower, they both grabbed a towel from the towel warmer and passionately rubbed each other's naked skin.

While Danielle was drying her hair, Zayden went into the bedroom, lit some candles, and turned down the covers on the bed. When he looked up from the bed, he saw Danielle staring at him. She gracefully walked up to him and gave him a longing kiss, and the heat of their bodies began to clash. He then picked her up and slowly laid her on the bed. "I've been waiting for this," he whispered. "So have I; it's all I thought about on the way here," she replied. He pulled her close as he laid down on her warm body. They shared a beautiful night of lovemaking. The fire between them ignited, reaching a more intense climax as they enjoyed a blissful night of fun.

Chapter 24

Weeks have gone by, and Raven was agitated regarding the delays in the closing of her house. The inspection was completed, and the buyer's agent was informed of two recommendations regarding items in need of attention or repair. She indicated that her client would not close until they were addressed or corrected. Either Raven would accept the inspector's report and follow through, or she would have to start from scratch for another buyer.

Raven had seven days to have everything done before there would be a reinspection. She wasn't willing to crash and burn, not at this point anyway. She contacted professional contractors to complete all the items. This delay was clouding her plans to get back to Chicago to continue her mission regarding Eric. Instead of the three to four weeks originally initiated by the buyer's agent, it was now the eighth week with no resolution.

The inspector returned and went down the list to reinspect. He confirmed all of the items had been handled and told her he would forward the information to the realtor as soon as possible. He signed off on the addendum and printed her a copy in his truck for her records. He later faxed a copy to the realtor, who contacted Raven hours later. She confirmed she had spoken to her client, and they were all set. She also verified that the attorney's office would contact her with a rescheduled date for closing within the next day or two. Although Raven was getting impatient about the entire ordeal, she gave her best persona and replied, "That's fine," and thanked the agent for calling to let her know.

The professional moving trunk arrived on time, and the team made the packing comfortable and stress-free. Her neighbors, who were piercing out of their windows, were completely unaware of her move, and they didn't bother to ask since she had been through so much. Finally, everything going back with Raven to Chicago was packed and ready to go. Everything else she wanted to keep was put in the storage facility. She gave many items to Goodwill and the homeless shelters in the area.

Harold and his daughters' family returned from their trip, and he was surprised Raven had not closed on the house. She explained everything that had delayed the process. Harold replied, "Yeah, I understand. The same occurred to me when I sold my last home. Things happen sometimes, and you have to be patient." "Oh, I know; that's what I've been doing," Raven said. I have stayed here at your house for the past two weeks. The closing attorney's office called today and set up a new date, so if you don't mind, I need to stay with you until then because the house is empty. "Oh, Sis, you know you're always welcome. Whatever you need. You're my only sister, and I love you," he replied. "Thank you," Raven quietly said. "Well, since you're here, would you like some dinner?" Harold asked. "Sure, how about something fun, like pizza, honey chipotle chicken wings, and a liter of Coke?" she laughed. Just place the order; I'm buying. "Oh, you're buying? Well, alright then, I would love to, he replied as he got down on his knees in front of her." She laughed and said, "Boy, if you don't get up off your knees," She grabbed an arm and helped him up. Harold pulled his phone out of his pocket, found the website, and clicked on each food item.

Within an hour, the food arrived. They sat at the kitchen table, devouring slice after slice, laughing, and reminiscing about their childhood. They talked about the time when Harold got the last slice of pizza and slipped it into his bed in the middle of the night. He was eating it so fast that he started choking and had to crawl to Mom and Dad's room for help. Harold laughed and said I got one for you. Remember when you put Mom's new high-heeled shoes in your bookbag and took them to school? You tried to walk in them, and fell down the steps, and broke one of the heels? The principal had to call Mom because you bruised your knee. "I remember that," Raven said, laughing. Mom put me on bathroom cleaning duty for weeks. They laughed so hard about the good times as well as the bad times. While cleaning up the kitchen, they were still laughing. Raven said, "That's the best time I had in a long time." Harold replied, "Me too, Sis." They hugged each other and retired to their bedrooms for the evening.

When they got up the next morning, Raven decided she would go visit her niece and her children with Harold. His daughter, Kathy, answered the door and was surprised to see her aunt looking so much better than the last time she'd seen her at her son's funeral. "Auntie, you look so good," she said. How are you feeling?" "I'm feeling good," Raven answered, smiling. "I guess I shouldn't expect anything less," Kathy commented. You are a very strong woman, isn't she, Dad?" Harold responded with a nod. They all sat down, and Kathy offered them something to drink. Raven talked about her time in Chicago and her plans to return when she closed on her home.

Kathy looked surprised and asked her, "You're not staying here?" "No, honey, I really enjoyed Chicago when I was there. There are so many places that I haven't visited yet, and I have a list of things that I want to do while I'm there," Raven replied. Besides, it's been very therapeutic for me, you know?" "I understand," Kathy commented, nodding.

"I miss Eric every day," Kathy said, looking a little sad. Did you have any difficulty settling up his affairs there?" "No, everything went smoothly," Raven replied. Some transactions took more time than others, but otherwise, everything went well. "That's good; one less worry for you," Kathy concluded.

As their conversations continued, Raven received a call from investigator Tim Connors. She excused herself and went outside to answer the call. He contacted her weekly with updates and what he had uncovered thus far, but had to dig a little deeper to conclude his findings. The homeowner, who approved Raven's application, contacted her about the rental. She explained to him how she would be delayed but promised she still wanted to rent. Satisfied with her request to hold it, he agreed and requested she contact him when she returned to Chicago. "Hello, Mr. Connors. Have you concluded your investigation?" she asked. "I have, and if you have some time, we can discuss it," he said. Whispering, Raven replied, "I'm not in Chicago right now and with some family members, so can I call you back later this evening or tomorrow?" Raven asked. "Sure, that won't be a problem. Just call me back when you're ready. If I'm not in the office, you can reach me on my cell," Tim said. "Okay, I'll call you back," she said.

Raven hung up and returned to her family, giving them an excuse. "That was the closing attorney confirming the date. I suppose they want to be sure that I'm present and on time." Harold and Kathy acknowledged her and continued their conversation. After talking for a while, Kathy invited them to dinner she had prepared, which was more than enough for all of them. They ate dinner and then sat back, continuing their talks about family and friends that Raven didn't even know.

Smiling, Raven walked over to where the kids were playing a game. "What's the name of that game?" Raven asked. It's the Uzzle, the kids said. The kids asked if she wanted to play. Raven declined. She said she just enjoyed watching them play. They would change to different games and laugh and talk at the same time. Raven listened to them talk about school and their friends until they were completely worn out. Kathy and her husband, Robert, put the kids to bed and then walked Raven and Harold to the door and said their goodbyes. Even though everyone was tired, it turned out to be a great day for a family reunion.

On their way home, Raven said to him, "Harold, Kathy has a beautiful family, and her kids are so much fun and polite." "They sure are, aren't they?" he replied. I have them over at the house sometimes to give her and Robert time alone. I learn something new from them all the time as they get older. "I'm sure you do; time has really changed since we were kids," Raven replied. "Yes, it has," he said. The kids keep me young, so they are my babies too, he smiled. They walked into the house, dragging their feet. Raven plopped down on the sofa and took off her shoes. Harold turned on the TV, grabbed a bottle of wine and two glasses, and sat down on the sofa. They shared the wine but consumed only half of it before bed.

After another week, it was finally closing day. Harold went along with Raven for support. They sat in the lobby of the closing attorney's office until Raven and the buyer were called to the conference room. Everyone was there. Raven and Harold, the realtor, the buyer, her husband, and the closing attorney. Raven had several documents to read and sign, and the buyer had a lot more. It took nearly an hour and a half as the assistant to the attorney made copies of the final signed documents for both Raven and the buyer for their records. Raven passed the keys across the table to the buyer, and everything was concluded.

When leaving the attorney's office, Raven took the two of them to lunch, and after placing their order, she pulled out her checkbook, wrote Harold a check for $5000.00, and passed it over to him. "What's this?" he asked as he looked at the check. He was in shock. "Raven, you don't have to do this," he said with tears filling his eyes. "Yes, I did," she replied. You have done so much for me in the last few months, and I really appreciate it. Do something nice for yourself.

"So, when are you leaving?" Harold asked. "Today is Wednesday, so I thought I would wait until the weekend if that's okay with you." "Of course, it's okay; you don't even have to ask," he said as he pulled a handkerchief from his pocket to wipe the teardrops from his eyes. I'm going to miss you, Sis. Take care of yourself. If you need me, know that I will be here for you. "I know you will, big brother. You have never let me down," Raven commented. Raven never knew Eric contacted Harold when he was on the run and that he was the one to alert the Chicago police of Eric's whereabouts. Harold knew she would never forgive him but instead would have made every effort to hide him herself, as she was very protective of him due to his mentality.

They finished the ride home and changed their clothes. Harold went outside and started weeding and watering his garden. He also dug holes for the new plants sitting in trays on his enclosed back porch. After making a few phone calls, Raven walked out on the back porch and watched Harold work in his garden. Something you just can't leave in the past, she thought to herself.

Raven walked out of the door and assisted Harold in his garden, picking tomatoes, cucumbers, green peppers, and cabbage for the remainder of the day. After the sun went down, they both came in and took a shower. They warmed the food that was brought home from Kathy's house. After eating, Raven went to her bedroom to read, and Harold went to prepare Raven's car for travel.

It was 5 a.m. Saturday morning, and Raven showered and dressed for the road. Harold checked her car and gassed it up the night before. She was packed and ready to return to Chicago. Before she got on the road, Harold cooked her a couple of eggs and bacon and made coffee. Afterward, he made sure everything was secure in her car and nothing was rattling around to cause her any distraction on the road. When he opened her door, Raven turned and gave him a huge hug, a tear falling from one of her eyes. Harold managed to say in a crackling voice, "Have a safe trip, Sis. Call and let me know that you arrived safely." "I will," she replied. Raven backed out of the driveway and got on the highway to make her way back to the Windy City.

On Friday, Raven had mapped out a timetable and alerted the owner of the home in Chicago she'd planned to rent that they would meet as soon as she got there. Constantly, Raven was reminding herself that she must attend to every last detail if she wants to carry out her brilliant plan. After a few hours of driving, her mind begins to wander about the rental property, the investigator's report and what it entailed, and thoughts of her son. All of a sudden, Raven's sinister side emerged, bringing a venomous sneer that saturated her face with pure evilness.

Chapter 25

Kim's due date is nearing, and the excitement of baby Carlisle is brewing with her and Xander. The room is complete, awaiting the arrival of the little girl or boy. Each time they attended Kim's doctor's appointment, the couple would come closer to finding out the gender but would back down when asked. As the due date approaches, the appointments become more frequent. Kim continues to work in her studio a little at a time as her military police husband, as Kim refers to him, watches over her. Diligently, she adheres to his orders and those of her doctor.

Isabel has been performing exceptionally well since her arrival. She has consistently maintained Kim's dietary regimen, and they are deeply grateful for this. Despite Kim's special diet, Xander hasn't missed any of Isabel's delicious meals. Kim has noticed his bulging abs since her pregnancy. "Well, well, mister, you're starting to look as pregnant as me," Kim said, patting him on the stomach. "It's not that bad, is it?" he asked with concern. "No, honey, I'm just kidding," Kim replied. "Don't worry, when the baby comes, I will be getting back to my regular workouts, especially since we have a home gym. It seems you thought of everything when we built this house, " Xander commented.

So, I suppose the baby duties will be all mine, huh?" she teased. "Nah, I'll change a diaper or two," he said, smiling. "I am going to hold you to it too, mister," Kim replied. "No, really, sweetheart. Laying all jokes aside, we are in this together, and I will put in as much time as you need me to. I will not be known as a husband who runs from his responsibilities," Xander said seriously as he took and kissed Kim's hands. Kim shook her head, smiling at him.

"Now, is there anything that you need?" he asked. "No, we're fine... Oh yes, and let Isabel know we will both be having salads this evening with unsweetened iced tea," Kim said. "Sure, okay," Xander said, cringing with a smile. "And no dessert," she said. "Got it," he replied. Xander saluted Kim and went off to do as instructed with a smile.

The phone rang. It was Kim's parents calling. "Hi Mom, what's up?" Kim cheerfully answered. "Your dad and I were just calling to see how you guys were doing," Janie commented. "We're doing great, Mom," Kim responded. Let Daddy know too. "I'm here, baby girl." I hope we're not bothering you guys too much," James said questionably. "No, Daddy, we understand; in fact, we welcome your calls. And if it's any consolation, Xander's parents call us weekly too," she said, laughing, hoping to ease her father's guilt feelings. "Well, the baby will be coming soon, and we can't wait," James said.

Kim smiled as Xander walked into the room. "It's my parents," she whispered. "Oooh," he whispered back. Tell them that I said hello. Also, our appetizer, as Xander called the salad, is ready. "Okay, I'll be right there," Kim replied. Mom and Dad, Xander, said to tell you guys hello. We're about to have dinner. "Alright, sweety, we'll let you go. We love you both," Janie said, and James chimed in.

Xander and Kim sat down to dinner. He looked down at the plate of the beautiful salad Isabel created for them, then up at Kim. "You're going to enjoy it, honey, and you'll thank me later; trust me," Kim said, laughing. "I'm sure I will," Xander said hesitantly. They proceeded to eat, and surprisingly, Xander enjoyed the salad but begged Kim for wine instead of the bitter concoction, which he refers to as unsweetened iced tea. Kim shooed off him with her hand and smiled an okay, nodding her head.

While Xander went to get a bottle of wine from the wine fridge, Kim said, "We should give Isabel a bonus. She has worked so hard for us, and I think she deserves it." "I agree, and I thought the same thing a few days ago. I was going to discuss it with you. So, what amount do you think we should give her?" he asked. "Well, she is with us nearly 100% of the time, and I'm sure she would like to be able to do something nice for herself. She takes care of her family's needs and ours; sometimes we all need some me time.

My idea is to treat her to a spa day and a nice meal at a restaurant of her choosing for her and her family. And to top it off, we can give her a check for $500 just for herself," Kim suggested. "That sounds great, sweetheart!" Xander said. After selecting a date for dinner and the spa, let's discuss it with her. But first, we need to check with Danielle to see what day she will be available. Keep in mind that we need someone with you just in case I go to the office or run errands. "Okay, I'll check with Danielle, and we'll speak with Isabel afterward," Kim commented. "Then it's settled," Xander said. Isabel will be so surprised. And she deserves all the quality time we can offer her.

By the way, this salad was filling, especially with the wine. He smiled. "I'm sure," Kim contently said, sipping her tea. They finished the rest of their salad as Isabel entered to remove their plate and check to see if there was anything more they needed. They thanked her for dinner and said they would retire for the evening. Isabel nodded as they got up to leave the dining room. They retreated to the bedroom, and Xander helped Kim to the shower. Once they were finished taking their showers, they got into bed and fell asleep for the night.

Chapter 26

The weekend had gone by quickly. Zayden and Danielle made every effort to spend as much time with each other as they could before she returned to Chicago. They visited a nearby mall for sightseeing and saw a movie. Afterward, they walked hand in hand down North Grand Street toward Nordstrom. All of a sudden, Zayden's sneaky eyes and face begin to glow with excitement. He guided her to turn left, where both of them walked into a three-level store. At that moment, Zayden surprised Danielle with a shopping spree. Danielle was in pure shock. As she shakily chose an item, she would show it to Zayden for his approval. Instead, he asked, "Is that for me or you?" They both smiled and gave each other an affectionate hug.

After a long day, they decided to skip an extravagant dinner and instead enjoyed a home-cooked meal prepared by Zayden. The menu consisted of baked chicken, fresh creamed spinach, corn on the cob, freshly baked cornbread, and Country Time lemonade. Naturally, the aroma from the different flavors begins to permeate all the rooms.

Danielle came down the stairs, sniffing. "Boy, you got skills," Danielle said, surprised by the elegant Bone China table setting in the dining room. "I forgot the lemons, so I hope you don't mind," Zayden said. "I don't care; I like Country Time lemonade," Danielle said, laughing. The dining table was draped with a gold-rimmed linen table runner, gold-trimmed dinner and bread plates, and crystal glasses under a beautiful chandelier. He had chosen slow jazz music for the evening.

When they sat to partake in the delicious meal, there was little conversation, and if it wasn't for the music, you may have been able to hear a pin drop. Zayden knew the two of them were thinking about the end of a wonderful weekend. His scheduled work-from-home days the following week were Monday and Tuesday, so he didn't stress about a late Sunday night. Playing with her food, Danielle looked up from her plate with sadness in her eyes. "I knew this would happen," she said. I really don't want to leave you in the morning. Since Zayden would work from home the following day, Danielle convinced him that she could take an Uber to the airport instead of interfering with Zayden's early morning work schedule.

"Why don't you change your flight and stay a few more days?" Zayden suggested. I'm working from home for the next two days anyway. "But I don't want to be in your way," she said in a forlorn voice. He gave her a look that said, "Really?" "No, you wouldn't, sweetheart," he reassured her. I don't have any meetings scheduled until I return on Wednesday, so we can spend some time here if you don't mind me working a few hours in between. I do get breaks and lunch," he said, winking an eye. It's not much, but at least we'll have that time. "Well, I do have a couple of classes scheduled, but it wouldn't be the first time I've had to cancel, which hasn't been in a long while. I think that my patrons can survive until then," she said. "Then it's settled," Zayden commented.

"Excuse me for a moment as she got up from the table. Since they're his regular off days, I will see if my second-in-command, Rodney, wouldn't mind coming in those days. I'll let him know that I won't be back in the gym until Thursday and to change my schedule. He actually loves it when I give him more responsibility outside of his personal trainer duties. I'll just tell him I'm taking some mental health days and request he handle things until I return," Danielle replied, looking positive. Zayden continued his meal while she left to make the call.

Danielle returned to the table with a huge smile on her face. "He was more than happy to take over while I'm out," Danielle happily said. I told him I would pay him since it was short notice, and I would give those days back to him the following week, but he said it was not a problem and was happy to do it for me.

You know, Zayden, I believe he still feels bad that he didn't stay with me the night I was attacked, as he usually did. He always walked me to my car, but that night it was snowing heavily, and I told him to go home because I had some paperwork to do. Tears filled Danielle's eyes as she relived that night. "It's okay, baby," Zayden said as he quickly got up from the table to console her. "I don't know if I'll ever forget that night, you know?" she whispered. "You will; it will just take a little more time than you probably expected," he said to her with concern.

Come on, let's finish dinner. I'll open a bottle of wine when we finish, and then we can relax and continue to listen to the music. "Okay, I'm sorry to bring up that horrible night," Danielle apologized. And I certainly didn't mean to put a damper on this beautiful dinner. By the way, it tastes wonderful!" she said in high spirits, even the yellow stuff. They both burst out laughing.

After clearing the table, washing, and putting the dishes away, Zayden grabbed a bottle of wine and two glasses, and they sat down to enjoy it. Danielle removed her shoes and sat back comfortably under his arm, stretched out along the top of the sofa. They engaged in small talk teasing, kissing, and listening to the sounds of legendary jazz artist Miles Davis.

Since Danielle wasn't leaving the next day and Zayden would be working from home, there was no need to rush the evening. A few hours later, they fell asleep. Danielle stirred, and Zayden woke up, looked around, and gathered himself. His sudden movement woke up Danielle. "We are bummed out," Zayden said. Let's go to bed, he announced. He helped her up, and they walked up the stairs slowly so as not to fall because the wine had made them a little tipsy. They bypassed the shower, got straight into bed, and fell fast asleep.

Danielle woke up early Monday morning. She did what women do when they feel that sexual urge. Passionately, she looked over at Zayden and began rubbing her body against his. Her touches aroused him. It took only a few seconds before he responded. When they started to kiss, their bodies heated up so quickly that they never noticed the chill in the room. Gradually, he got on top of her, and they engaged in the highest degree of profound intimacy.

After a few minutes of talking, they got up, took a shower, and dressed. Zayden powered up his computer but didn't start to work until after they had breakfast and coffee together. When Zayden started to work, Danielle excused herself from his office and called Kim. She and Xander had finished breakfast, and he was on his way out the door to go to the office for half of the day.

Danielle told Kim that she was staying at Zayden's for the weekend, but it turned out that she stayed longer than anticipated. Kim said, "I wondered why we couldn't reach you or Zayden." She laughed. It wasn't that hard to put two and two together. "I take it that I don't have to ask if you're having a good time either, do I?" Kim smiled as she asked. "I'm having a great time. Zayden has been so hospitable," Danielle said, sounding elated. I'll be home on Wednesday, though. "Good, I need to ask a favor, but it can wait until you get back," Kim replied. "Sure, no problem; I'll come by Wednesday afternoon once I get settled," Danielle said. "Great! Xander and I will see you when you get back," Kim replied.

Danielle and Zayden enjoyed each other's company and made their time together last a lifetime. He drove Danielle to the airport early Wednesday morning. Zayden planted a longing kiss on her before she left for her flight to Chicago, a kiss that would keep them together until they saw each other again.

Looking out of the airport windows, Zayden watched her plane as it taxied to the runway and lifted into the air as he slowly walked through the corridor of the airport. Exiting the airport doors, Zayden knew he should settle his mind and get his attention back to the office workday ahead.

Chapter 27

After driving for hours in unexpected traffic jams on her way into Chicago, Raven returned in time to meet with the landlord of the house she was renting. She was on an adrenaline rush. After ironing out all the particulars and signing the lease, Raven called investigator Tim Connors, whom she hired, to see if she could see him as soon as possible. He was not in his office, so she called his cell.

"Mr. Connors, this is Raven Wilder (using her maiden name). "Hello, Ms. Wilder, I hope you're doing well," he replied. "I am, but I'll be doing better when I get your report. I am eager to move forward. How soon can we meet to discuss the findings of your investigation?" she asked. "I'm at an appointment right now, and it's getting late. My wife hates it if I'm late for dinner. We can meet in my office early in the morning; if that will be okay with you," he questioned. "If that's the best you can do, okay," Raven commented, annoyed. That bonus, if there is one, just got reduced, she thought.

Right now, Raven has become ruthless. She had time to think on the way back to Chicago and was ready to do what she had to do to sever her son's memory. Her plan wasn't complete without the investigator's report, but she had to calm down and be patient for Eric's sake.

She took time to unpack her car and organize the home she would occupy for the next few months. She ordered delivery for dinner due to the weariness she now felt from the drive.

I suppose the adrenaline has worn off, she said, laughing to herself once she sat down.

The evening she originally planned for herself was short because of the declination of the investigator. After dinner, she took a well-deserved, long, warm, and relaxing bubble bath. Afterward, she dressed for bed, puffed up her pillows, and propped herself up to gather her thoughts. Tomorrow will be a busy day, and Raven was preparing herself for what would be revealed in the investigator's report. In some ways, searching for information about someone she had never met exhilarated her. And for her, she hoped there would be something in the report that would help her get what she needed to carry out her plans.

Raven awakened refreshed the next day. After a good night's sleep, she realized her patience was well worth it. She had her morning coffee while thinking about the information the investigator had obtained. Afterward, she dressed and drove herself to his office. When she arrived, Raven was escorted to his office, where he was awaiting her presence. He waved for her to have a seat and handed her a copy of the file.

Raven opened the file to review what was inside. She lifted the pages one by one, reading each one carefully. With eyebrows raised, she said, "Huh, so Ms. Casey was engaged before." I see that the ex-fiancé is a little down on his luck. He's working as a handyman. Really? "That's what we found," Connors replied. As you read on, you'll learn that he lives with his girlfriend and their five-year-old daughter in a low-income neighborhood. "I wonder what happened with him and Ms. Casey. I mean, why was their engagement broken off?" Raven asked. "From the information I gathered, Craig Carter—that's his name—was found unfaithful in their relationship, and Ms. Casey walked away.

Despite being caught red-handed, he also faced a substantial financial burden. Mr. Carter was in college and interning at the time but had to drop out because Ms. Casey was no longer around, and his savings were dwindling quickly. He moved in with the girl he was caught with, but this did not resolve the issue. Mr. Carter ended up looking for work, and with only a high school education, he was not afforded corporate status anywhere. In fact, to this day, he is still working as a handyman to make ends meet. His girlfriend, on the other hand, is working at a fast-food restaurant," Connors said. "Well, I take it; he could use a little help, Raven thought to herself.

"And, Ms. Moore, I see she has an unsavory past as well," Raven commented. Connors replied, "Yes, but it's still unclear where the money came from for her to open Core's gym. She was raised in a drug-ridden neighborhood, where she engaged in drug usage and sales. The community was raided, but Ms. Moore got out just in time, which left me thinking that she either stole the money and fled or double-crossed an ally. She goes by her mother's maiden name of "Moore," but her birth name is "Alexander." "Now that's interesting," Raven commented.

"I've listed all past and current addresses of them all, along with current phone numbers and any other pertinent information," Mr. Connor reiterated.

And since Mr. Xander Carlisle is part of Ms. Casey's life, I included, at no charge, of course, his background as well.

As he pointed to the file, that is your copy to keep, Ms. Wilder. I hope that all my findings are to your satisfaction," Connors replied. Raven nodded and said, "Yes, yes, it is." "If there is anything else you need, please do not hesitate to call me," he said, rising from his chair. "Thank you so much, Mr. Connors. You have done everything I've requested and much more," Raven replied. She pulled out her wallet and paid Connors the remaining balance in cash, plus an additional $1000.00 as a bonus for his extensive efforts.

Raven would try once more to contact Kim, but this time to be honest with her about who she was and to see if she would respond to her request to speak with her about Eric. She would hold onto the information as a second resort if Kim denied her. Raven returned to the house, satisfied with her morning. She made herself a turkey sandwich, sat down at the table, and thumbed through the file once more, reading everything again, detailing and circling things she felt would be helpful to her. As she was reviewing, parts of the report had her shaking her head. And the media had them smelling like roses, Raven said out loud. I wonder what they would say if they saw this report, especially Danielle's past, she thought. She found it interesting to find out that her son dated her too. Raven shook her head once again and pondered, "I wonder if they both were working together, playing my son."

Raven was now aware of Danielle's connection to Kim. The longer she read the report, the angrier her thoughts became. Raven rose from the chair, put on her shoes, and went outside to get a breath of fresh air. As she paced the walkway, her thoughts started to switch back and forth between happy and sorrowful moments. Raven decided to take a walk to decompress and relax.

After a short walk, Raven came back into the house. She sat down with her head bowed and her hands entwined on her forehead. As a result of her anxious thoughts, she felt lightheaded and had no appetite. So, she repositioned her head on the leather couch and kept her eyes closed until she fell asleep. Around one in the morning, she woke up, took a shower, got into bed, and went back to sleep.

Chapter 28

Danielle arrived at O'Hara Airport earlier than expected. She had a few minutes before her rideshare arrived, so she called Kim to confirm that she would see her later that evening once she checked in at the gym and settled in at home. Kim agreed and told her Xander should be home by the time she got there. Danielle grabbed her bag from baggage claim and walked toward the airport exit doors for her ride.

She arrived at Core's and saw Rodney at the front desk. He looked up, surprised. "Hey, Ms. Moore! I didn't know you would be coming by today," he said. "Hi, Rodney, glad to see you too." Danielle smiled, shaking her head. How did everything go while I was gone?" "Everything went smoothly. You will be happy to know there were no problems at all. A few of the clients were a little upset that their classes were canceled, but others understood. If you ever need me to fill in again for you, I will be more than happy to," Rodney said. "Thank you again, Rodney, for holding down the fort. What would I do without you?" Danielle replied. "Hopefully, you won't ever have to," he commented.

Are you staying for the day? "No, I just dropped by to see how things were going and to put some things in my office. After making my way to the baggage claim, I felt a little jet-lagged and exhausted. I'm going home to get a little rest, then going by to see a friend of mine later this evening. You're welcome to take the day off tomorrow if you want to," Danielle added. "Nah, I'm okay," Rodney said. Would you like me to walk you to your car? "Sure, if you don't mind. But I can get one of the security guards to do that if you're busy," she replied. "I'm good. Are you ready?" he asked. "Okay, let's go," Danielle responded.

Danielle went into her condo, and the first thing she did was kick off her shoes, drop her bag at the door, and strip herself of her jacket. She then plopped down on the sofa and exhaled, sitting there for a few minutes before getting a glass of water. Danielle set her alarm for 4 p.m., then laid down to take a nap at around noon. She fell into a deep sleep, and before she knew it, the alarm buzzed. Rubbing her eyes, Danielle got up, took a shower, got dressed, and sat for a while before heading out to Kim and Xander's house.

When she pulled into the driveway, Xander was right behind her. He opened the garage door and waved at her as he drove in. Danielle parked and knocked on the front door. "Hi, Isabel, how are you?" she asked. "I'm fine; come in, Ms. Moore," Isabel responded. Have a seat, ma'am. Ms. Carlisle will be out in a moment. Would you like something to drink while you wait? "Okay, thank you, Isabel. And no, I'm fine," Danielle replied. By this time, Xander had walked in, and pleasantries were exchanged as Kim walked into the room. The two bear-hugged. "Well, how was your trip, Missy?" Kim questioned sarcastically. You look a little worn out. "If you must know, my friend, it was so much fun!" Danielle responded, grinning from ear to ear. "That must explain the worn look you have," Kim said. "Anyway, I brought you something back," Danielle said as she handed Kim a gift bag. Kim reached into the bag and pulled out a beautiful snow globe to put in the baby's room. It had a mother holding her newborn inside. "Thank you so much. That was so sweet of you," Kim said with tears in her eyes. You know you didn't have to bring us anything. "I know, but I wanted to," Danielle replied. If I'm going to be a godmother, I need to get a head start. They both smiled and hugged each other again. This time, tears fell from both of their eyes.

"What's all this?" Xander asked as he walked into the room after changing clothes. "Look at this, honey. Danielle bought this for the baby's room," Kim said, handing him the snow globe. "This is really nice, Danielle," Xander commented. Thank you. "You are both welcome. I couldn't come back and not remember my friends, now could I?" Danielle said. tilting her head and smiling. Now, what about your trip? Kim asked.

They sat down, and Danielle talked about her entire trip and Zayden's hospitality. Danielle described Zayden's home and all the fun they had sightseeing. Xander chimed in, saying, "Yeah, he bought it nearly a year ago." I haven't been to see it since he moved in, though. "You really need to see the inside of it, Xander. It is huge! In fact, it is a lot bigger than it looks from the outside," Danielle said. Your brother has it beautifully decorated, too. "That doesn't surprise me at all. He is a stud," Xander responded, smiling as he walked to the kitchen to see what they were having for dinner.

"Hey, Isabel, what's for dinner?" Xander asked. "I made something that you could all have. I prepared chicken broccoli pasta and garlic toast, salad, and lemonade," Isabel replied. "Yummy, yummy," Xander said, rubbing his hands together. "Everything will be on the table in about five minutes," Isabel commented. "Okay, I'll round up the troops," Xander said as he saluted her.

Isabel smiled at him, shaking her head. Xander took an antique bell off of the buffet. Walk into the living room, where Kim and Danielle are having a deep conversation. Being comical, he rang the bell, announcing dinner was ready. Laughing, Danielle said, "Well, he brought some life to the party." Kim laughed so hard that you could see the baby's feet kicking.

Still laughing, they all sat down to eat. Everything on the table looked appetizing and appealing. "Isabel is a real jewel, huh?" Danielle asked. Yes, she is. That's what we want to talk to you about," Kim commented. Isabel has been with us for a while now, and she is doing a great job. Xander and I thought we would gift her with a spa day and dinner for an evening for her and her family. "That's great," Danielle said.

Since I am so far along, nearing the baby's arrival, we wanted to know if you could stay with me on the day we chose for her. We wanted to discuss it with you before we surprised her. "You don't even have to ask twice," Danielle said. Whatever you need, I'll be here. You do know that I own my own business, she reminded them, smiling. "We know, but we didn't want to inconvenience you," Xander intervened. "Anything, anything at all for you guys," Danielle replied. Just let me know the day, and I'll adjust my schedule. I'll even do Isabel's part of the job if it's not too hard, she said, laughing. They all laughed and finished dinner, continuing their conversations about Danielle's weekend trip and the baby.

Chapter 29

Raven was awakened by the noise of a lawnmower and rubbed her eyes after a good night's sleep. It took her a moment to realize she was in unfamiliar surroundings. Still feeling drowsy, Raven forced herself to get up and walk to the kitchen to make coffee. While she sat at the kitchen table with her hands wrapped around the warm cup, Raven began to think of her plans for the day. She also reflected on the white lie she told her family by keeping the real reasons or circumstances surrounding her decision to return to Chicago. She knew they would have tried to stop her and attempt to get her to seek professional help, which her brother Harold suggested to her after she laid her son to rest. But she was determined that if she were to get the answers she wanted, it would be on her own merits.

Her first order of business would be to contact Kim at the number in the investigator's report, hoping she would speak with her regarding Eric. Given the heinous crime, she knew it would be a long shot, but at least she should make an effort. At this stage, Raven's thoughts lead her to blame Kim and her friend, Danielle. She felt their involvement with Eric was more than what she'd heard on the news, seen on social media, and read in trashy magazines.

Raven had a feeling that at least one of them was more than a friend because of the engagement ring found in the safe. She wanted answers, and if they made it difficult for her, the results would not be favorable for either of them. Raven would do whatever she needed to do to get the answer. And because the two were friends, Raven forced herself to keep a positive attitude and, in earnest, knew she had to try.

After a breakfast of bacon, eggs, and toast, Raven cleaned the kitchen and sat down with another cup of coffee, grabbing the report lying on the sofa and thumbing through it once more. She finished her coffee and picked up her phone to call Kim. Wiping her eyes, Kim looked at her cell on the nightstand and wondered who would be calling her so early. The number came up as private, and she thought that was unusual. Xander was in the shower, preparing to go into the office, so she went ahead and answered.

"Hello, this is Kimberly Carlisle, she answered. Raven paused before responding. She introduced herself as Eric Harris' mother, Raven, and asked to speak with her for a few minutes about Eric. Kim started to feel uneasy, and she had a questionable look on her face before she replied. "I'm sorry, who did you say you are?" "I'm Mrs. Raven Harris, Eric Harris' mother, Raven said with a slight irritation in her voice. You did know him, didn't you?" "What do you want? And why are you calling me? How did you get my number?" Kim asked nervously. "I want to know how well you knew my son," Raven replied. "To be honest, Mrs. Harris, or whoever you are, I don't think it was a good idea for you to contact me. I don't know how you got my number, and frankly, I don't care. So, please do not call me again," Kim said with strength in her voice as she hung up.

Kim's response upset Raven, and she slammed her phone down on the sofa. "Did that bitch just hang up on me?" she said out loud. She began to fume on the inside. Kim's hanging up on her made the matter go south really quickly. She thought that if she tried speaking with Danielle, the response would probably be the same. With that, Raven decided to put her plan into motion, but she would need to put some things in place before moving forward. She snatched up her phone, grabbed the legal pad and the file of information, and moved to the dining room table to begin putting her plan together.

Since Raven was unable to have a civil conversation with Kim as she'd hoped, drastic measures were now needed. She felt she was left with no choice. Raven knew Kim's ex-fiancé, Craig Carter, had money issues and may need money, so waving an attractive offer to him for assistance might work, she said to herself. Her anger had intensified. The next call she made would be to Mr. Carter.

As she sat back and thought about it, Raven had the look of a grinch about to strike. She read in the investigator's report that Craig had a resume on file with Indeed.com, so she would use that as her reason for calling and take it from there. She located his number in the file and proceeded to call him. The call immediately went to voicemail. She left a convincing message about a potential job offer, hoping it would get his attention and prompt him to call her back. She turned on the television for any interesting programming to pass the time away.

The home only had basic cable, so there wasn't much to choose from. After thumbing through a few channels, she found the western, Bonanza. She always loved watching westerns in her heydays. Bonanza ends with Ben recognizing what they've been through and swearing to tell his close friend the truth, and then the ending theme song starts, and, for a split second, it puts a smile on Raven's face. As she was about to watch The Big Valley, her cell rang. It was from the number she had called earlier for Craig.

"Hello," Raven said. "Yeah, someone called me from this number," Craig replied. "Yes, Mr. Carter, my name is Raven Harris of Enterprise Resource Planning, and I understand that you are looking for a position in management consulting." "Yeah, how did you know that?" Craig questioned. This boy is dumber than I thought he was, Raven deemed. "We ran across your resume on Indeed.com, sir," Raven commented. Are you still interested in this type of work? she asked. "Yeah, yeah, um...what do I need to do?" he replied excitedly.

"Reviewing your resume, Mr. Carter, I see you attended college. Did you complete your program to graduate, sir?" Raven asked. Raven attempted to sound as convincing as she possibly could to hold Craig's attention. "No, ma'am, I completed three years but was unable to finish college because my financial aid had run out and the Pell Grant monies were not enough," Craig replied. "Well, Mr. Carter, I have a 3-month position that could become a full-time position in the future, located in Chicago. Your expenses, of course, would be fully paid, including a rental vehicle, a hotel room, and a stipend to help pay for other expenses. The total pay for your time and services will be $6000, which will be paid separately. Does this interest you, Mr. Carter?" Raven asked. Craig couldn't believe what he was being offered and almost choked.

"Ms. Harris, what exactly does the position entail?" he asked in a questionable tone. "You would be given a list of art and interior design studios for placing orders and arranging pickups for a few hours per day," Raven answered. Due to the ongoing COVID-19 pandemic, designers are primarily using Zoom calls, allowing you to work from your hotel room using a company-owned computer. You will also need to be professionally dressed for all calls. Would that be a problem, Mr. Carter?" "No, no, I understand. You've answered my question.

So, what do I need to do now?" he asked. "Mr. Carter, you are needed right away, so we will arrange for you to catch Amtrak from your area into Chicago. How soon would you be able to leave to get here?" "I can get there as soon as possible," he replied. "Good, the arrangements will be made, and you will be texted the information. Once you arrive, a rideshare will be waiting at the station to take you to the Congress Plaza Hotel. When you get there, go to the hotel check-in. Give your name to the clerk, and she will give you the key to your room. Once you are settled, give me a call at this number, and we will go from there," Raven explained. "Okay, I will need to let my girlfriend know about the job and give you a callback," Craig replied. "I understand and will await your call, but Mr. Carter, don't take too long because others are looking for jobs just as you are," Raven commented. "I won't," he replied and hung up.

Craig could not contain himself and immediately told his boss that he had to leave for the day and went home to tell his girlfriend, Kate, about his new job and its location. She found the pay very odd and intensely questioned Craig. "Don't you think that's a lot of money for just three months of work?" she asked. "I know, but she found my resume on the job board for Indeed, and everything appears legit to me," he replied.

Kate was not happy that Craig would be away for the next three months, but she understood because they did need the money. Subsequently, Kate knew Craig's current weekly salary was just not cutting it, given he only worked 2, 3, or maybe 4 days per week, then worked odd jobs some days. She wanted so much more, and if this was a way, then she was on board. They made the most of his remaining days and prepared to say their goodbyes.

Craig called Raven the following day and told her he could leave in two days. Raven agreed and started making the arrangements for his stay, including going out to purchase a computer, preparing a fake list of designers, and placing Kim's studio at the top of the list. She felt Craig would gain a rapport with Kim after all these years and hoped her plan would work. Raven left nothing to chance and made her plan as real as possible. She completed all the arrangements, including the Amtrak ticket and rideshare, and texted Craig everything he would need, explaining his ticket would be at the station when he arrived. At last, everything was finally coming together.

Chapter 30

Kim was noticeably shaken when Xander walked into the room. She had a look of fear on her face, and her eyes were red and watery. Xander ran to her quickly. "Baby, what's wrong?" he asked calmly as he sat down next to her on the bed. Kim turned to look at him, and she could barely breathe a word. "Kim, baby, what is it?" Xander asked her again, seriously concerned. "Xander, she called," Kim said as tears fell from her eyes. "Who, who called?" he asked. "His mother," Kim said, whispering audibly. "What, whose mother?" "Eric's mom! ....She said her name was Raven Harris, and she wanted to talk to me about Eric," Kim said as her voice heightened in sound. "How, what, when?" Xander asked, as it was clear now why Kim was so shaken.

"While you were in the shower, my cell rang, and it indicated a private number. I questioned myself if I should answer since it was so early, but I thought maybe it was someone wanting to pick-up their painting. She practically demanded to talk with me about Eric. When I asked her where she got my number, she didn't say. She said she wanted to know how well I knew her son. I told her that I didn't think it was a good idea for her to call me. I then asked her calmly and politely not to call me again, and I hung up. I'm unsure if she will call again, but I'm scared, Xander, really scared.

"What if she believes I'm the reason Eric committed all those crimes?" she asked, shaking. "She won't, baby; I promise, she won't," Xander responded, attempting to assure her. "What should we do? Should I change my number?" Kim asked, now shaking uncontrollably. She was panicking and starting to hyperventilate. Xander did all he could to console her. The incident had been too much for Kim, especially now that the baby was almost due. At the moment, Xander decided not to go into the office but to stay with Kim so she would feel safe and secure.

Everything appeared to be going smoothly with them since they moved into their new home. Xander's pure happiness changed in a matter of seconds into his worst nightmare. Now, the dark thoughts have begun to enter his mind again. He helped Kim back into bed and had Isabel prepare some green tea. Xander was determined to ensure her safety, and he would do everything possible to prevent any potential harm.

Desperately, Xander had considered purchasing a firearm early on but never disclosed the information to Kim. He hesitated to buy it as he believed Kim might not approve of having a gun in the house. Lovingly, he made Kim a promise, and he aimed to keep her safe by any means necessary. Xander felt that if Eric's mother had Kim's number, then there was a possibility she may have her address too. "Why now, why now?" he murmured. His state of mind was confused, yet he was able to make rational decisions. Furiously, Xander was not willing to take a chance of letting evilness devastate her life again.

Once Kim finished her tea, Xander held her close until she fell asleep. He quietly slipped out of bed and went to speak with Isabel. He explained that Kim was sleeping and that he needed to go out for a while. He instructed her to keep an eye on Kim until he returned in about an hour or so. Isabel assured him that she understood and would frequently check on her without waking her.

Xander went out onto the patio and googled for firearm shops near their home. To his surprise, the closest was located in the Loop area of Chicago, near their office, which was farther than he thought. When he went back in, Kim stirred with panic, asking for him. Isabel ran to her side, as did Xander. "I'm here, sweetheart; I'm here," he said. Come on, lie back down, and get some rest, honey. I need to go to the office and pick up some paperwork, and I'll be right back. Isabel will be with you until I get back. "Do you have to go?" Kim cried. "It'll just be for a little while, I promise," Xander replied. I swear, everything will be fine. I will call you when I'm on my way back, okay, sweetheart? "Okay," Kim soberly replied. But come right back, okay? "I will, sweetheart; don't worry," he said.

Xander dressed and got into the car, leaving for the gun shop. He didn't show it in front of Kim, but he was upset that she was upset. When he arrived at the store, Xander walked in and went directly to the counter for assistance. A salesman approached and assisted him, asking what type of firearm he was looking for. Xander explained that he needed something that would stop an intruder in their tracks and be powerful enough to fatally injure, if necessary. "I've got just the thing," the salesman replied.

From the glass case, Xander was shown 40-caliber Smith and Wesson clips and revolvers. He took his time looking them over and handling each for weight to make his decision. Once he decided, Xander completed all the necessary paperwork. The salesman explained that the National Instant

Criminal Background Check would be necessary and that it would take about 48 hours to complete. Xander acknowledged his understanding and requested prompt notification for pick up.

The salesman then questioned if he would need assistance in the operation of the gun. Xander replied, "No, that's ok, I've got this," he said as he reached for his wallet. The salesman nodded. Xander made his purchase along with additional ammunition, just in case he needed it.

He got in his car and called Kim, as promised, to confirm he was on his way back. Anticipating the worst, he could feel and hear there was some calmness in her soft-spoken voice. The short phone call ended with, I love you, and I will be there soon. With a half smile on his face, Xander decided to stop by the florist to pick up some fresh-cut flowers, knowing they would perk her up even more and put a smile back on her face.

Chapter 31

Officer Simms, the chief investigator for the Marcus Blackstone case, is always on the job, and he noticed that lately, Marcus's list of visitors has increased. Simms's quick wit and keen eye have kept close tabs on that list in the last few months. Marcus was an unsavory character, and Simms felt there was more to him than just the Thomas Eric Harris fiasco. He knew Blackstone had other cohorts out there creatively keeping him supplied with information from the outside, but nothing had panned out thus far. Simms generally scans the list about twice every 2-3 months, and the same family members seem to visit Marcus. They would come, stay a few minutes, and place money on his books for writing paper, postal stamps, cigarettes, snacks, etc.—nothing out of the ordinary.

Except for one day, as Simms reviewed the list, he was surprised to see Harris' mother, Raven, had come to visit him weeks ago and left a hefty sum of money in his commissary account. His curiosity peaked as to why she would visit someone who was involved in criminal acts and alert them to her son nearly being captured.

Simms's instincts kicked in with interest, and he was intrigued. This was something he was not going to let go of, at least not just yet. He thought to himself that, as a courtesy, he would give Raven a friendly "hello" to see if maybe he was onto something, although he thought it to be unlikely but worth his time to confirm his curiosity. He would also check in on Xander and Kim Carlisle. Simms knew they had a baby on the way because of all the excitement among Chicago's elite and also the talk of the Chicago circuit.

Immediately, Simms returned to his office and sat down behind his desk. He leaned in on his desk with both arms and hands intertwined against his mouth, looking straight ahead. I wonder what the two of them talked about, he said to himself. Was it something important? Alright, don't let your mind run away with this, Simms thought. There is one way to find out: ask the source himself, Simms said out loud. He quickly called the jail to have Marcus brought to his office right away. Maybe, or maybe not, he would get answers, but it would be a start.

About twenty minutes later, an officer arrived with Blackstone in handcuffs. "Thank you, officer," Simms replied as he pointed to the chair in front of his desk for Blackstone to have a seat. "So, what's up, doc?" Marcus questioned. Simms exhaled, rose from his desk, and shook his head as he stood directly in front of him and said, "You are the same low-life thug we brought here over two years ago. I see nothing has changed with you at all." "Never mind the semantics investigator, WHAT DO YOU WANT?" Marcus asked.

"I want to know why Raven Harris came to see you," Simms replied. "Why do you wanna know?" Marcus asked, sitting handcuffed sideways on one arm of the chair. "No reason; just wondering why she would come to see you, of all people, that's all," Simms said. "Maybe...she...wanted to say "hi," Marcus replied with an attitude stretching his neck upward. "Okay, that was it?" Simms asked, putting his arms behind him and leaning back on the desk, looking straight into Marcus' eyes. "That's it," Marcus said. Look, man, what is it that you're looking for? "Nothing, in particular," Simms calmly said.

"What if I told you about what we talked about? Would that get me some time off my sentence?" Marcus said, trying to strike a bargain. "Now, you know that's not going to happen," Simms commented as he pushed himself up from the desk, crossing his arms. I can get you more time out of your cell a few times a week, as long as you give me something useful, but not before. Marcus sat up straight, licking his lips with his head down.

"Ms. Harris wanted to know about the women Eric was involved with," Marcus recalled. "Oh, so you call her Ms. Harris?" Simms asked. "It's a respect thing," he replied. I've known Ms. Harris ever since I was a kid. Anyway, I told her. I don't know why she wanted to know after all this time, but she did. "So, she asked you about Mrs. Carlisle and Ms. Moore?" Simms asked. "Yeah, man, that's what I said," Marcus said, frowning. "Wonder why she would ask you?" Simms inquired. "Maybe because she heard that I screwed one of dem," Marcus replied, smiling and leaning back with his hands in front of him. She wanted to know where she could find her, cuz she already knew where to find that girl ya boy was banging. "Huh, do you know why she wanted this information?" Simms asked with a curious expression. "Man, who knows? I just told her what she wanted to know," Marcus said.

"Okay, okay," Simms said, nodding as he walked behind his desk to buzz for the officer to return. "Mr. Blackstone, thank you for your time," he said. "What about…" but before he could finish, Simms told him he would put in the order for the additional time. The officer removed Blackstone from the room and returned him to his cell. Simms sat thinking for a while. Why was she asking Blackstone questions? I wonder if she's still here in Chicago.

His curiosity about Raven Harris strengthened. Then he picked up the phone to call Ms. Moore on her cell. "Hello," Danielle said. "Hi, Ms. Moore, It has been a while; this is Investigator Simms; how are you?" "I'm doing very well, and yourself?" "Great, still busy getting the bad guys," he replied. "I want to thank you again for everything you did to catch the man who attacked me," she continued. "All in a day's work," he said. They both laughed.

"Ms. Moore, the reason I'm calling is that I was wondering, has the mother of Thomas Eric Harris contacted you?" "No, not that I know of; I can't say that I have," Danielle replied. Why? Is there something wrong? "No, I was just curious. I understand that she may have been in town for whatever reason," he said. "Oh, maybe she's visiting a family member or something," Danielle said nonchalantly. "Maybe," Simms replied. Well, you take care of yourself and have a good day. "I will, and thank you for calling," she said. "You're welcome," he said, and they ended their call.

Simms continued by checking the number in his folder. He put his finger on the name Xander Carlisle and dialed his number. "Hello, Xander Carlisle here," he said. "Yes, sir, this is Investigator Simms. How are you and Mrs. Carlisle?" he asked. "It's strange you should ask. My wife received an unusual call from the mother of Eric Harris a couple of days ago, but the number came up as private. It scared the hell out of my wife," he explained.

Although she is fine now, the fear in her eyes has made her so afraid for her life. "She's about to have a baby, you know," Xander asserted. And what's more bizarre about the whole situation is that we have no idea how she got Kim's cell number or why she felt she could call her. "Did she say why she called?" Simms questioned. "Yeah, Kim said she wanted to talk to her about her involvement with Eric, but she told her it was a bad idea that she called her and asked not to call again. "Do you think she will?" Simms asked. "I hope not, because Kim doesn't need the stress, especially now," Xander said with concern. "Alright, Mr. Carlisle, keep vigilant, just in case. I don't understand why, after all this time, she would return to Chicago and contact Mrs. Carlisle when she could have done this from her hometown.

Furthermore, I have no idea if she is still in Chicago or, if she is, why. Please contact my office if she calls again," Simms responded. "Yes, we will," Xander replied. Do you think there's any cause for concern, investigator? "I don't know yet, but I just have a feeling. I guess it comes from being an investigator all these years, he said, smiling to himself. "You just seem to pick up on things sometimes. It's just the instinct in me, I suppose," he said. "Well, take care, and best wishes on the arrival of your new baby," he beamed. "We will. Thank you for your kind words, and we appreciate all of your help, Investigator Simms. I'll let Kim know you called," Xander stated.

After saying their goodbyes, Xander laid back in his chair with his hands over his eyes, wondering how much he should reveal to his sweet, loving wife. It seemed like every time they had peace, something came along and interrupted their joy. He didn't want Kim to be upset again. So Xander decided to hold off and seek out additional information from other sources.

Chapter 32

Craig arrived in Chicago on Amtrak right on time. He exited the station, and as Raven confirmed, a rideshare was awaiting him. As instructed, the driver drove him directly to the Congress Plaza Hotel. When he arrived at the hotel and stepped out of the car, Craig was in awe of the well-dressed man standing near the door, waiting to greet him. He entered the room, immediately drawn to the crystal-bright lights surrounded by opulent architectural trim. The hotel staff promptly informed Raven of his arrival.

Craig walked to the hotel desk and was given the key. He then went up the elevator to his room. When he opened the door, he was amazed at its spaciousness and luxurious décor. Craig had no idea that the room would be a huge suite, fully equipped with everything he would need. Raven set the desk up for work, and the laptop was there, loaded with the Enterprise Resource Planning software. Raven spared no expense. She planned to only have the room occupied for, at the most, three weeks if everything went as planned.

Craig unpacked, then took a shower and rested a while before calling Raven. After a short nap, he got up and walked over to the floor-to-ceiling window, admiring all the large, architectural buildings in the far distance. The richness in the atmosphere gave him a euphoric feeling of success and happiness. Slowly, Craig's mind drifted back to reality, and he sat down on the plush sofa to call Raven.

"Hello, Ms. Harris. This is Craig Carter." "I see you arrived safely, Mr. Carter. Are you ready to get to work?" she asked. "Yes, ma'am, I am," he replied. "Since you just got in, you can have the rest of the afternoon to enjoy your surroundings, and I will be there at 9 a.m. tomorrow to personally introduce myself and to welcome you to Enterprise Resource Planning. I left some cash under the laptop for you to enjoy a nice dinner and maybe explore some of the beautiful sites in this city of Chicago. You'll receive your stipend tomorrow when I arrive." "Yes, ma'am, thank you," Craig replied. "Have a good evening, and I'll see you in the morning," she said and hung up.

Craig checked under the laptop, and there was $500.00. He still couldn't believe what was happening to him. He promised himself that he would be a model employee, in hopes that the job would become a full-time position for him and his family.

Craig doesn't have a clue or any idea of the plans Raven has in store for him. He believes he was chosen out of many others for a position that would make him more money than he could ever dream of or imagine.

Craig face-timed his girlfriend, Kate, after speaking with Raven. He described the accommodations Raven set up for him and showed her the entire room as he walked through. "That's really nice, Craig, but are you sure about this? Aren't you curious about any of this at all?" she asked, very concerned. I mean, really, who is this woman? "I told you, Kate. She heads a consulting company and needed some help in Chicago for a while. Don't you realize the money I'll be making could solve all our money problems?" he pleaded. "I understand. It all sounds good and everything. It's just... something doesn't feel right about any of this. But if you're okay with it, I'll stand behind you, but Craig, be careful. Chicago is a huge city. "Okay, baby, I will. Now, let me go so that I can go out and get some food. I haven't had anything to eat since I got here this morning," he explained. I'll call you when I get a moment tomorrow. "Okay, talk to you soon," Kate replied with intense concentration. And Craig, don't forget what I said; be careful.

Craig didn't mention the large sum of money Raven left for him to spend that day, or she would have been beside herself, he thought.

Craig walked out onto the bright lights of the Chicago streets, looking around at all the many eateries and restaurants near the hotel. The hotel had a nice restaurant, but he wanted to get out and get some fresh air. He walked down one street, then up another, until he came to Magrinis, a restaurant and bar. Curious, he walked into the place, playing soft music. The bar was located on the left, and tables for dining were on the right. He was approached by Matre'd Andre', who took him to a very nice table and handed him a menu.

Everything on the menu looked quite expensive, but he recalled that Raven had left him enough money to treat himself to a nice meal. Craig ordered a medium-well T-boned steak, asparagus, and baked potato with a glass of white wine. He added a slice of key lime pie to take with him back to his hotel room to enjoy later with something from the mini bar. Craig felt like he was living the life of the rich and famous, taking advantage of everything available to him.

Early the next morning, Raven arrived with a briefcase and a folder in her hands and was pleased to see Craig professionally dressed as required. She turned on the laptop and explained to him the software spreadsheets. Raven then provided him with the first directory of designers' businesses and instructed him to make Designs, etc. his contact for the day. He was instructed to order two small abstract paintings and advise the owner, Kimberly Carlisle, that they would be needed in two weeks. Craig nodded, confirming he understood. Raven never revealed that his ex-fiancé was the owner of the studio. She then advised him to confirm with the owner that he should be called when they were ready, and arrangements would be made for the pickup.

Raven handed Craig a cell phone and made it clear that it was for business use only. She told him that he could make his private calls from the phone in the room, if needed. He was not, by no means, to use his cell phone for business. "Now, do you have any questions?" Raven asked. "Yes ma'am. Do you want me to continue with the directory once I've completed the order with Designs, etc.?" Craig asked. "No, not today. I want to make sure you can handle the first order before we move on," she replied.

Sometimes, it takes days to connect with designers about what is to be ordered. Craig looked directly at her and dropped his head, indicating he fully understood. "Also, Mr. Carter, the calls will be on Zoom, so you will first call the offices, where they should set up a time with the design owner and send you a link for your meetings. This may take them a day or two."

An email account has been set up for you, as she handed him a custom business card with the company's logo, his email address, and business number printed on it. "Be sure to check your email often for messages from me and designers that are contacted." Raven reminded him. "Yes, I understand," he responded. She handed Craig a beige envelope with a custom navy-blue logo printed on the back. "This is your stipend for the week, and I will call you later," she said as she opened the door to leave. Enjoy your day, Mr. Carter! He said thank you, and you too.

When Craig closed and locked the door, he was jumping for joy, like he had just won the lottery. With the logo and the stipend, Craig knew now that this job was truly legit. Soon, he can shop for special gifts for his family, and he can't wait to hear their voices when they receive them. Maybe this will prove to Kate that we are on the right track for living a better life.

Raven confirmed the details for ordering from Kim's studio when setting up her plans. She knew Kim was working from home and only utilizing Zoom to speak with her clients and confirm pickups.

Chapter 33

Raven came out of the Congress Plaza Hotel and stood in front of the revolving doors, deciding which direction she wanted to go. The sun bounced off the gold trimming of the hotel into the streets and nearby buildings. If anyone had turned their head to look directly at the glare, the sun's powerful light would have rendered them blind. As Raven walked closer to the curbstone, she could see the streets were bustling with people shopping, dining, and sightseeing. She could also see a makeshift Ferris wheel and other attractions in the distance.

When she crossed the street, Monica, Kim's administrator, and her husband, Jay, were sitting in a little bistro having lunch a few feet from the hotel. She looked out of the window to her left while talking with him and was stunned to see Raven coming from the direction of the hotel. She watched as she walked toward a traffic light on the corner of the street. Monica stops Jay in the middle of their conversation and points out the window. "Jay, look!" she said, nearly scaring him out of his wits. "That's Eric Harris's mother right there!" she said in a loud whisper.

"What? Where?" Jay appeared confused. Looking around, he finally focused his eyes in the direction Monica was pointing. "She's a long way from home. I wonder what she's doing here in Chicago," she said to Jay. "That is strange... unless she has some business here," Jay said, attempting to be the voice of reason. "Really?" Monica commented with her lips pursed. I don't mean to sound paranoid, but I don't have a good feeling about this, Jay. Do you think we should let Xander and Kim know she's here in Chicago? I don't want them to be blindsided. "I know, honey, and it may be nothing," Jay said, trying to make light of the situation. Looking at Monica's face concerned him.

"Maybe it would be a good idea," he said. "You really think so?" Monica said, exhaling a sigh of relief. "Yeah, it couldn't hurt. It's better to be safe than sorry," Jay replied as Monica smiled back at him. "Okay, I'll give them a call when we get to the truck," Monica commented.

They continued talking and finishing their lunch, then walked down the West Loop to his truck in a parking deck. As they were approaching the entrance, they saw Raven coming out of one of the high-end clothing stores with two shopping bags heading in their direction. They stopped and turned away, pretending to be in conversation. Glancing downward, Raven didn't notice them because she was too busy rearranging her bags and purse in her hands.

Monica and Jay waited for a while until they could see her leave. Once they saw her exit the parking deck, Monica immediately pulled out her phone to call Xander and Kim. Jay asked her to wait until they got to the truck. When he opened the door for Monica to get in, she was visibly shaken as she dialed Xander's number. "Calm down, honey; it's going to be okay," Jay said, putting his right arm around her shoulders.

"Hello... Xander? Hi, this is Monica," she said at rapid speed. "Slow down, Monica, Xander chuckled. What's wrong?" "You are not going to believe who Jay and I saw a few minutes ago downtown," she said. "Who?" Xander said it nonchalantly. "Eric's mom, Raven Harris!" she said nervously. "Really?" Did she say anything to you?" Xander anxiously asked. "No, she never knew we saw her; why?" Monica said as she stared in shock at Jay. "She called Kim's cell phone a few days ago, and it really got her upset. She wanted to talk to her about Eric, but Kim refused, and she asked her not to call back again. We have no idea how she got Kim's number. I had a feeling that she was here somewhere in Chicago, Xander commented. "We first noticed her crossing the street from the Congress Plaza. Jay and I thought it would be best if you both knew," Monica said, with her voice still trembling. By the way, how is Kim doing? I haven't spoken with her in a few days. "She's fine. I'm trying to keep her from worrying so much," Xander replied. Otherwise, we are just waiting for the big day. So are we, Monica said, with Jay smiling in the background.

I just wanted to let you know that while watching Raven, I got anxious and nervous. Jay said that maybe she had business here, but I didn't have those same feelings. Especially when I saw she had made purchases from one of the high-end clothing stores near the parking deck at the West Loop.

You know, Monica, it's probably best that she didn't see you since you were there in court when her son was sentenced so many years ago. "Yeah, I guess you're right. I'm glad we took the precautions we did.

Well, we won't hold you. We just wanted to give you a heads-up, Monica commented. "Thanks, Monica, and please don't mention this to Kim when you talk to her. I want her to stay calm, okay?" Xander asked. "Sure, no worries.

That's why I called you instead," she said. Give Kim our love. "I will; we'll talk with you guys later," Xander said.

Xander hung up the phone, feeling more than ever that something wasn't right. He was now convinced that purchasing the firearm for their protection was a good idea. Kim was not aware of the purchase, but he did inform Isabel since she already knew what happened to Kim many years ago. Before hiring Isabel, her background check stated that she was an experienced firearm owner.

When she was hired, she wasn't allowed to bring any type of weapon into the house. That's why Xander spoke to her about his purchase privately and explained to her that it would be in a combination gun lock box and stored in the China cabinet drawer. He gave her the key to the cabinet drawer and the combination to the gun lock box for safekeeping. Xander instructed her to keep the key nearby, especially when he was not home. She nodded and said, "Don't you worry, Mr. Carlisle, I understand."

On his way to check on Kim, Xander remembered Monica saying they saw Raven near the Congress Plaza. He stopped in his tracks and pulled out his phone to call his friend, Dominic, who investigated Eric Harris for him when Kim was attacked. He walked back down the hall to go outside on the patio to make the call.

"Dominic," "Hey, man, this is Xander," he quickly said. "Well, that's a name I hadn't heard in a while. How's it going, bud?" Dominic questioned. "We're good. How is your family?" Xander asked. "Everybody's good. Damien just turned 12, and the little girls are swarming around him like bees in a hive. Maggie is 5 now and has quickly emerged into the girly girl stage, where everything must be pink. When we go shopping, she must go from store to store looking for *Barbie* pink. You just wait; your time is coming." They both burst out laughing.

I know this is not a social call, so what's up?' Dominic asked. "You remember Eric Harris, the guy who attacked Kim years ago?" Xander asked. "Yeah, how can I forget? That was a bad time," Dominic recalled. By the way, how is she doing? "She's taking it easy. You know our first little one is on the way, right?" Xander asked. "Are you kidding? All of Chicago knows," Dominic said, teasing Xander. Sorry, we couldn't make it to the wedding. Sarah's mom was sick, and we had to fly to Washington State that weekend. We still owe you guys a gift, though. "No, you did me a huge favor years ago that I won't forget, which brings me to why I called," Xander said with concern in his voice.

"What can I do for you?" Dominic asked with a serious tone. "Eric Harris' mother is here in Chicago," he said. She called Kim a few weeks ago, wanting to talk to her about Eric. Of course, Kim refused, but the call really shook her up. "Oh no!" Dominic shockingly said. "Dominic, what I need for you to do is find out where she is staying and what she's doing here. I want as much information as you can find," Xander explained.

Kim's administrator, Monica, and her husband, Jay, saw her yesterday near the Congress Plaza Hotel. Maybe she's staying there. It's just a hunch. "Not a problem, buddy. I'm taking a couple of days off anyway, so I have time to get on this right away for you," Dominic replied. And don't you worry; I got this. I'll let you know what I find out as soon as I can. "Thanks, buddy. I really appreciate it," Xander replied.

Xander felt relieved and heaved a huge sigh before walking back into the house. Isabel caught him before he went to check on Kim to let him know that dinner was ready. He told her they would be there in a few minutes. Xander pondered as he walked down the hall to get Kim for dinner. When we finish dinner and Kim is settled in bed, the next step is to contact Investigator Simms to let him know Raven is in Chicago, Xander thought to himself.

Chapter 34

Xander called Investigator Simms and alerted him to Raven's presence in Chicago. "A couple of friends of ours saw her yesterday in the downtown area, possibly leaving the Congress Plaza Hotel. They later witnessed her coming out of one of the high-end clothing stores. Simms, why do you think she's here?" Xander asked. "That's a good question," he replied. "So, I mean, what can we do?" Xander asked. "Honestly, Mr. Carlisle, there is nothing we can do. She's here, and no crime has been committed. So, until something occurs that involves her criminally, our hands are tied," Simms explained.

What I will do is put an officer in the area to patrol periodically, and if anything comes up or if anything seems suspicious, we will notify you immediately, sir. Xander took a deep breath and said, "If that's all you can do, I guess we'll just have to be vigilant." "I understand your concern, Mr. Carlisle, and I promise you that we will do everything we can to keep you and your family safe. And again, let us know if she calls again. "I will," Xander said as he exhaled.

Dominic called Xander after a few days. "Hey Dom, how are you? Did you find anything on Raven Harris?" he questioned. "More than you know, my friend," Dominic replied. "To be honest, Mrs. Harris is certainly up to something. She has been in Chicago for a while now and is using her maiden name, "Wilder," for whatever reasons.

Your employee, Monica's instinct was right on the money. Mrs. Harris has a suite in her name at the Congress Plaza, but she is not occupying it. I thought about checking to see who was actually in the suite, but I didn't want to cause suspicion. I also confirmed that she paid cash for an entire month. I was informed that she comes and goes occasionally. I went to the hotel, sat for half a day, and saw her come in. She was there for about thirty minutes, then left. I followed her to the Lake Oak subdivision, where the houses are priced in the high $700,000 range.

Additionally, Mrs. Harris rented a house from a man who is temporarily living in Florida. When I investigated further, I found out she recently sold her family home in Michigan. It appears she had been in the area for months before leaving to go back to Michigan and then returning to Chicago. Seriously,

I don't know what her angle is or what she's up to, but I suggest you be on alert. "Can you fax me the report of your findings?" Xander asked.

"Sure, not a problem, but better yet, I can drop the file by your office," Dominic suggested. "That would be great!" Xander replied. I will be in the office tomorrow until noon. Would that work? "Definitely, I'll be there around 9 a.m. and leave the sealed envelope at the front desk, if that's okay," Dominic said. "Sure, that will be fine. And Dominic, thank you, man. Let me know what I owe you," Xander replied. "It's on the house, my friend. You take care and let us know when the baby arrives. If you need anything else, I'm just a phone call away, he said. "Will do, Dominic. Thank you so much for doing this for me. I'll talk to you later."

While Kim was sleeping, Xander went to the family room and sat down to reflect on the information Dominic had revealed to him about Raven Harris. "Wilder," he said to himself. I wonder why she would disguise herself using her maiden name. His natural investigative curiosity began to grow stronger. Clearly, something is wrong with this scenario. When he receives the file from Dominic, he will notify Simms again and let him know what he has uncovered. In the meantime, he knew to be careful, as Dominic suggested.

The next morning, after having breakfast with Kim and talking about their plans for the day, Xander told her to call if she needed anything and that he should be back around 1:00 p.m. "If you would like for me to bring you something for lunch, give me a call on my cell phone," he said. "I will, and don't forget to pick up something sweet for the baby," Kim said. "For the baby, or for you?" Xander teased. "For the two of us, how about that?" she giggled. "Okay, sweetheart. Make sure that you get some rest while I'm gone," he said. "Don't I always?" Kim smiled at him. Now go to work and get back here as soon as you can. "I will see you later, and let Isabel know if you need anything, okay?" "I will, now go," she said.

Xander arrived at the office, and Dominic had already been there. Cathy, the receptionist, handed him the envelope left for him. Xander thanked her and asked that she hold his calls for the next hour, unless it was Kim or their housekeeper. "Yes, sir," she responded. Xander then went directly to his office and closed the door behind him. He put down his briefcase and took off his jacket. The envelope had a company logo sticker on the front and back and was tightly sealed. He pulled out a letter opener from his desk to get it open, and then sat down to review the report.

After going back and forth, he formed a list in his mind of Raven's comings and goings, including when she called Kim. He pulled out a legal pad and began compiling a detailed chronological timeline. He planned to contact Simms as soon as he finished and reveal what he had uncovered. Xander was determined that if Raven Harris, or whatever she called herself, had any plans of causing havoc or hurting his family in any way, he wanted to get in front of it now and make sure he stopped her before things got out of hand.

As he read page after page, Xander realized Raven had been roaming the streets of Chicago for months—in fact, nearly six months—before returning to Michigan. He continued reading to get an idea of when she came back and rented the house in Live Oak, or why she returned to Chicago at all. Xander began to feel uneasy, maybe because Raven had already made one attempt to talk with Kim. Not knowing her reaction to the rejection made him slightly anxious and nervous. He knew he had to do everything he could to protect his family. The police, at this point, weren't doing enough to investigate Raven, leaving him perplexed on what to do next. As he stared at the legal pad, he felt helpless and alone in finding a solution to this ever-growing nightmare.

Suddenly, Xander's attention shifted to Zayden, his brother and best friend. Their brotherly love is built on a foundation of shared childhood experiences, teenage secrecy and sports, and, as adults, respect for each other. Also, they have supported and encouraged each other through the good, the bad, and the ugly. Fortunately, he knew that Zayden was just a phone call away and would listen to him and understand his sense of impending danger. Exhausted, Xander gazed up from the legal pad and slumped back in his chair before drifting off into deep thought.

Chapter 35

To satisfy his curiosity, Investigator Simms took a trip to the reservation desk of the Congress Plaza Hotel to get the room number and as much information as he could about Raven Wilder. With the room number written on a hotel business card, Investigator Simms went up the elevator to the room and knocked on the door. Craig had just called to schedule an appointment with Designs, etc. designer Kimberly Carlisle for a Zoom meeting to place a project order. Cathy, the receptionist, advised that he would need to speak with Monica, the administrator, but that she was out of the office at the moment. Cathy took his name and number for Monica to return the call.

Craig quickly got up from his desk chair and opened the door, thinking it was Raven checking in but instead shocked to see Simms, dressed in a nice suit and raising his badge for identity. Craig stuttered. "Uh... can I help you, officer?" he asked nervously. "Don't be alarmed, sir. I'm Investigator Simms of the Chicago Police Department, and I'm checking to make sure all the patrons are safe here at the hotel. There was a shoplifter earlier at one of the downtown clothing stores. We received a tip that he may have entered the side door of the hotel. We wanted to make sure everybody was safe. "Yes, sir, I haven't heard anything unusual, but I will keep an eye out for any suspicious person," Craig said as he calmed down.

Without provocation, Craig added, I'm just sitting here working. "If you don't mind me asking Mr. Umm...," Simms hesitated. "Carter, sir, Craig Carter," Craig replied. "Yes, what is it, Mr. Carter, that you do to keep you working in a hotel room?" Simms inquisitively asked. "Oh...well, sir, I am a marketing consultant for Enterprise Resource Planning. I just started a few days ago. Actually, I commission artwork from various interior designers in Chicago. "Oh, I see.

Is the owner also here in the hotel?" Simms asked. "No, sir," Craig replied. She comes by daily to check and see if everything is going well," Craig said nonchalantly. "I wanted to know so that we could check on her as well. By the way, what is her name?" Simms asked. "Ms. Harris, Mrs. Raven Harris, sir," Craig sputtered. "Thank you. Well, as I explained, Mr. Carter, we're checking on all the guests in the hotel, so I will kindly let you get back to work," Simms commented in a firm voice. If you see or hear anything suspicious, please contact the hotel desk. "I will, sir," Craig replied as he closed the door.

After speaking with Craig, Simms felt a flashing sense of urgency that made the hair on the back of his neck stand up. He was almost sure Raven Harris was targeting Kimberly Carlisle, but why?" he thought, recapping over in his mind what he knew thus far.

Raven Harris has an expensive suite in a hotel and is not occupying it. Instead, she has an employee living and working there. She sells her home and rents a high-priced house here in Chicago. It's probably more than what she needs or can afford, and she now has a consulting business. "What is wrong with this picture?" he asks himself.

Simms returns to his office. He then called in another one of his investigators and assigned him to check out Harris's business, Enterprise Resource Planning, and requested that he need the information as soon as possible. Subsequently, Simms picks up the phone to call Xander and explains the shocking news he has uncovered about Raven Harris. "So, I was right," Xander said. "Maybe, but we don't want to get ahead of ourselves," Simms commented.

Has your wife received a call from Enterprise Resource Planning? "Why?" Xander asked in a quavering voice. The reason I asked is because this so-called employee said something that leads me to believe he has or will be contacting her. "Not that I know of," Xander replied. "I don't want to alarm you just yet, Mr. Carlisle, but I believe Raven Harris is setting up something to get to your wife, and soon," Simms explained. I'm not sure if I'm right. At this point, it's just a gut feeling. Do me a favor, check with your office, and call me back, he asked. "Sure, I'll call you back in a few minutes," Xander quickly said.

Xander called the office and spoke with Monica, asking if an appointment had been set for a Zoom meeting with Kim. Monica asked him to hold on for a moment while she checked her messages. "Yes, here we are," she said. Cathy received a message from Craig Carter with Enterprise Resource Planning requesting a Zoom meeting to commission some art pieces, but I haven't had the opportunity to check Kim's calendar to schedule him yet. I was going to schedule the appointment later today. "Okay, thank you, but hold off until I call you back," Xander said. "Sure, is there a problem?" she asked. "I don't know yet. Just wait for my call," he sternly said. "Okay, Xander, no worries," Monica assured him.

Xander then returned Simms's call and confirmed Kim's office had been contacted by Mr. Carter with Enterprise Resource Planning, but Monica had not called him back yet to schedule the meeting. "Great!" Simms reacted. Do you think you could have your office stall for a day or two?" he asked. "Sure, but what are you going to do?" Xander asked. "I don't know yet, but I'll be in touch with you tomorrow," Simms said. "Okay, I'll wait for your call," Xander replied, sensing Simms was holding back on some important information. "And Mr. Carlisle, please do not alert your wife just yet. I want to make sure that I am on the right track in my thinking, okay?" Simms asked. "Sure, okay," Xander said.

Xander thought about his strategic plan to keep his family safe. He knew that he had to be careful, so he would wait for Simms to call him back. In the meantime, he would work at home for the next day or so to be close to Kim.

So far, Kim has been relaxed and calm, and he is determined, with all of his heart, to keep it that way. Having good friends who have stayed connected with them has also helped a lot during those turbulent days. Monica calls Kim every week, and Danielle calls and visits often. Those calls and visits not only keep Kim in high spirits, but there is no longer a mention or conversation about the infamous phone call.

Chapter 36

A couple of days went by, and Xander hadn't heard from Simms, so he decided to give him a call. "Investigator Simms is here," he answered. "Yeah, this is Xander Carlisle," he replied. What's going on? I haven't heard from you, and it's been days. "Mr. Carlisle, you must be patient, sir," Simms told him. We don't want Ms. Harris to catch on to anything that would raise a red flag. Believe me, we have watchful eyes on her. We have various unmarked cars patrolling her subdivision inside and out, as well as any visitors that may arrive at her home. We're doing everything to stay a step ahead of her.

By the way, I was planning on calling you tomorrow. Simms interjected. "For what?" Xander asked. Can you go ahead and have your office contact Mr. Carter and set up the Zoom meeting with your wife?" Simms asked. Do you have a day in mind?" Xander inquired. "I would like for you to schedule the meeting in the next few days," Simms replied.

Also, I believe it's time for your wife to know what's going on. I would like to sit down with both of you to devise a plan prior to the Zoom meeting. "How soon can we meet before then?" Simms calmly asked. "Well, first, I need to tell Kim what we've been doing," Xander explained. I want her to process what I'm about to tell her, because upsetting her is the last thing I want to happen. She's weeks away from delivery and had considered putting future projects on hold until after the baby is born, but she does have a couple of approved art pieces for owners who are currently out of the country. They won't be picking them up until after returning to the States late next month.

"Okay, whatever you say, Mr. Carlisle, but the sooner, the better," Simms stressed. We want to do this smoothly, without incident, if possible. "I understand," Xander replied.

After hanging up, Xander had to think of a way to approach Kim with the information he and Simms had acquired on Raven. This is not going to be easy, he thought, but it has to be done. It was getting late, so he decided to sit her down after breakfast in the morning and explain everything, then contact Monica to set up the Zoom meeting with Mr. Carter.

Simms's investigator knocked on the door. "Come in, Chuck," he said. "Here's the information you requested, sir, regarding the business of Raven."

Simms opened the file and scanned the notes. He then looked up at the investigator. "Is this right?" he asked him. "Yes, sir," Chuck replied. I'm about as surprised as you are.

"So... Raven Harris' deceased husband worked for a company with the exact same name over 25 years ago, and it went bankrupt 10 years ago," Simms emphasized. "Yes, sir, it sure did." I double-checked. And get this, sir, the husband was an executive and was linked to a money laundering scheme within the company. "What!" Simms bellowed. "Yes, sir, this family has a long history of some type of psychological disorder.

According to these records, Mr. Harris was clearly a deranged and delusional man. "Chuck, this is getting better and better," Simms said, scratching his head. You did a good job getting the answers to the many questions I had rolling around in my head. Thank you for being so thorough and concise. "Not a problem, sir, will there be anything else?" Chuck asked.

"Yes, regarding this employee named Craig Carter. He's working for her, but I'm not sure if he is aware of what she may be capable of. Get me a background check on him, and quick! Simms shouted. And Chuck, call me as soon as possible when you get it! "Yes, sir, Chuck said as he left quickly, slamming the door behind him.

"Oh, my God, everything this woman has been through has got her mind as twisted as her husband and son," Simms said audibly. Damn, what in the hell are we dealing with here? I think I need a drink, he said to himself, rubbing the back of his neck as he got up from his desk. Simms picked up the file and put it in his briefcase, wondering how much more he would find out about Raven and her family.

After a long day of trying to put the pieces together in a complex criminal investigation, Simms went home, took a long, warm shower, and got comfortably dressed. The warm water had revitalized his body, but he needed a drink to stimulate his mind. So, Simms walked over to his small corner bar and poured himself a cocktail before sitting down to review all the notes in the Raven Wilder Harris file.

As he turned the pages one by one, he could not believe the documented information he was reading. He now knew he had to be more careful than he first thought. At this point, he didn't think that he should involve Mrs. Carlisle, given her condition. Disturbingly, there are so many questions about Raven's state of mind, and he did not want to take a chance with Kim and her unborn baby's lives. Subsequently, he turned his thoughts to her best friend, Danielle Moore, and wondered if she would be willing to help them. It was a long shot, but he needed to make the change.

Simms called Xander and asked that he invite Danielle Moore to their meeting. "Why?" Xander asked curiously. "I will explain everything when we meet," Simms replied. I know this is a last-minute request, but I have a good reason for my investigatory request. "Okay," Xander said hesitantly. I'll give her a call tomorrow. "Good, then I will meet with all of you later," Simms said, and he hung up.

As hanging up, his phone rang. It was the investigator, Chuck. "What did you find out, Chuck?" Simms asked desperately. "Boss, you are not going to believe this. Craig Carter is the ex-fiancé of Mrs. Carlisle," he said. The relationship was broken off years ago due to his indiscretions. "So, Harris must have had this information prior to seeking him out for her plans," Simms said, speculating.

The first scenario is that he may be either completely in the dark or not aware of what she's doing. The second scenario is that she could be using him as a pawn in her scheme to get to Mrs. Carlisle, or third scenario, he could be working right alongside her. In all of these scenarios, she must be paying him handsomely. "Yes, sir, and Mr. Carter has been living it up around town, spending large sums of money," Chuck added. Is there anything else, boss? "Yeah, email me that complete report right away. "Yes, sir, anything else?" Chuck asked. "No, Chuck, you did a great job. This is all I need for now," Simms replied. Thanks a lot. I'll see you in the morning.

Simms went back to the table, where he had the file of information spread out. He then scratched the top of his head, asking himself, "Why is this woman here, and what does she want? He sat down and closed his eyes with his head down in his hands. What could she possibly be up to, he thought? Again, he started to recall the information in his head.

This woman has set up shop in a city that she is not that familiar with, in a hotel room, no less, with an employee of the ex-fiancé of someone she doesn't know. This woman and her employee are running around town, spending large sums of money. And this woman has a twisted mind and is mentally unbalanced.

Simms kept going over and over this in his head. After a while, he quickly opened his eyes and looked up. She can't be, Simms said to himself. That's it! What other reason could there be? Raven... Harris... is... out... for... revenge, he shouted. That's it! That's it!, That's it, he kept saying. She is targeting the Carlisle family. Simms gathered up all the information, feeling he now knew Raven's motive. He went to his computer and printed an email report about Craig Carter, then put everything in his briefcase.

Chapter 37

Raven arrived at the Congress Plaza Hotel to check in on Craig. He was still dressed and standing at the windows, watching the sunset and listening to the sound of the television in the background. She knocked on the door, which broke his concentration. He opened the door, surprised to see Raven standing there.

"Good evening, Ms. Harris," he said with a confused look. How are you as she walks in? "Good evening, Craig," she replied. How are things going? "Okay, I guess," he said, exhaling. I haven't heard back from Designs, etc., and it's been a few days now since I made the call. Do you think I should call them back? "No, give them another day and see what happens, okay," she replied. "Yes, ma'am, okay," he said, nodding his head.

"So, have you been taking in the sights of beautiful Chicago?" Raven asked. "Yes, I sure have. I didn't realize there were so many places to visit," Craig said excitedly. I've done some shopping for my girlfriend and my little girl, and I thought I would go ahead and send everything to them to enjoy now. I miss them so much. "I know—it's hard to be away from those you love for such a long time," Raven sympathized as she thought of Eric.

"To be honest, Ms. Harris, I don't know if I want to continue these assignments after the contract ends in three months," he sadly said. And with the economy, there is no way we can afford to relocate here. "I understand how you feel, Craig," she said. Hopefully, we can wrap this up within three months, so you'll be able to get back to your family sooner. "Now, that sounds like a winner," Craig replied, smiling.

Raven was sure someone would have responded by now. She would delay her decision for another day before making any changes to her plans.

"Oh yeah, by the way, there was word of a shoplifter possibly roaming around somewhere loose in the hotel yesterday. Officers went door-to-door checking on hotel guests, but apparently they didn't do anything because I never heard anything further. "That's good; hopefully they found the culprit," Raven said indifferently.

"Now, you look a little bored. Would you like to go downstairs to the lobby for drinks and dinner?" Raven asked in a motherly tone. Everything is on me.

"I sure would like to go because the walls in this place are starting to close in on me, not that I'm complaining about the room," he laughed. "Then, let's go," she said.

They walked into the restaurant and sat at the bar. Raven expressed to him that he could have anything on the food and drink menu. The bartender came over to them and asked, "What can I help you two with tonight?" She looked up from the menu and said, "Bring me a bottle of champagne and a glass." Craig replied, "And I'll have a glass of white wine.

As the bartender walked away, Craig turned to Raven and asked in a bewildering voice, "Are we celebrating something, Ms. Harris?" "No, I just wanted to splurge a little. And I'm also feeling a little restless these days," she replied. "Oh, okay," Craig commented. The bartender returned with the champagne and Craig's glass of wine. He popped the champagne bottle and poured a glass for Raven.

"Are you guys having dinner this evening?" the bartender asked. "Yes, but give us a moment or two, please," Raven commented. "Not a problem; I'll come back in a few minutes," he replied. They looked over the menu to decide what their taste buds would enjoy. It appears they were in synch since both decided to order the same meals: medium-well sirloin steaks, broccoli, and red-skinned mashed potatoes. The two sat for a few hours talking about Craig's family and friends, but nothing about Raven's personal life except for work.

After dinner, they continued to sit and drink a while longer. Craig had consumed three glasses of wine and a couple of beers when his eyes began to burn, turn red, and become droopy. He knew it was time to leave, but he didn't want to impose on his boss's relaxation time. Raven continued to enjoy herself by finishing the bottle of champagne and then ordering a glass of red wine. By the end of the evening, they were both feeling a little tipsy but decided to go back to Craig's room for a nightcap.

Once they settled on the sofa, they moved from discussing the work and the money he could make to having Raven slither all over him and caress him in places that aroused him. He looked surprised but needed sexual stimulation due to Katie's distance from him. Smiling up at him, Raven began to loosen his belt, rubbing against his private part while mumbling her words in slow motion. "I know it's been hard for you to be away from home," she said. So, why don't we have some fun together to forget that void in your heart and loneliness in your soul?

Raven then unloosened his tie, unbuttoned his shirt, and unzipped his pants. She kicked off her shoes, stood up, removed her dress and undergarments, and walked over to the king-size bed, which surprised him even more. Suddenly, Craig was nervous about what was happening and asked, "Ms. Harris, do you know what you're doing?" "Boy, of course, I know what I'm doing," she replied. Now come on. I know you need this, so come here and get it. Craig breathed a huge breath, hunched his shoulders, and walked over to Raven, removing his clothes.

Passionately, she began to kiss him, and he was partially reluctant but eventually obliged. She went in on him fearlessly, like a lion, and he could feel she needed him more than he would ever know. Raven performed sexual acts that Kate had never done, and that alone surprised his loins. She was enjoying every inch of his body; that didn't faze him at all. He laid there, mesmerized by his emotions, and the mere fact that Raven was a much older woman than what he was accustomed to made him more receptive to her every command.

The sex went on several times during the night. He was surprised at Raven's drive and tenacity. She slowly rolled him over and got on top of him. Raven was stroking him much more than Kate could ever handle, almost wearing him down and out. Craig couldn't believe the energy she had, given that she was so inebriated, but instead, he laid there enjoying it all. All of a sudden, they both moan loudly as they climax at the same time. Raven kissed Craig and rolled to her side of the bed. They both drifted off, not knowing each other's thoughts.

Raven woke up before the rising of the sun, looking around the room, then at Craig, quietly sleeping. Reality hit her as she looked and saw that she was completely naked. "Oh, my God! She whispered. What the hell was I thinking?" she asked, chastising herself. Feeling a little remorseful, Raven quietly eased out of bed and quickly took a shower.

When she got out of the shower and dressed, Craig stirred but didn't wake up. Raven quietly picked up her shoes and grabbed her jacket and purse, then quietly opened the door and slowly slipped out. Without a sound, she gently closed the door behind her.

Outside the closed door, she put on her shoes and jacket and quickly left the hotel. She still could not believe what had occurred between her and Craig.

He was old enough to be her son. Raven felt bad for a while but later started to feel empowered. She had not engaged in sex since her husband died.

Being with Craig reminded her how powerful and liberating it felt to be loved. In a way, Raven was feeling very accomplished, but she didn't lose sight of why she was in Chicago. Knowing it would be awkward and uncomfortable, she decided to check in with Craig later in the day.

Chapter 38

Everyone awaited Investigator Simms to arrive, except for Xander. They were puzzled as to why he would want to see them all together. They thought of various scenarios, but nothing made sense. While they were having coffee, Isabel answered the doorbell chime. After viewing Simms's image on the camera, she opened the door. "Come in, Investigator Simms," she affirmed. Everyone's waiting for you in the great room. "Thank you," he replied as he followed her.

As Simms appeared in the doorway, Xander stood up to acknowledge him. "Good morning, everyone," he stated. I suppose you're wondering why I wanted you all here. "Yes, we are," Kim was quick to answer. "Ditto," Danielle piggybacked. "What is it?" Kim asked.

"Why don't we all have a seat?" Simms requested. I asked you here because I have some news, and you may find it disturbing. "Simms, you are making me nervous," Kim said. Xander noticed her nervousness getting stronger, and he immediately went over to Kim and took her by the hand. "Mrs. Carlisle, I have reason to believe Mrs. Harris is here in Chicago targeting your family as revenge for her son, Eric," he said firmly. Kim gasped, putting both hands over her mouth. "But why?" she asked, barely able to hold it together.

"To be honest, Mrs. Carlisle, I'm not sure where her head is at this point, but she has launched a bogus business, Enterprise Resource Planning, that is set up in one of the suites of the Congress Plaza Hotel. She has only one employee. I took steps to disguise my intentions when speaking with him.

Honestly, the young man never suspected or sensed why I was there. In fact, we had a great conversation about the company's name, his job description, and how long he worked there. After reiterating about the shoplifter, we ended our discussion with a handshake and a smile.

As I was walking toward the elevator, a red alert sign started blinking in my head. When I got to the elevator, I realized his description of his responsibilities struck me as weird. "What was it?" Kim asked as she began to panic. Xander held her tight. "He is going to commission pieces of art from your company," Simms replied. Apparently, Mrs. Harris has done her homework and is aware that you are working from home, and all pieces would need to be picked up from your home.

"Where did she get this information?" Xander asked. "We are not sure, but it could have unknowingly come from your office," Simms answered. I have taken steps to have her activities monitored round-the-clock, but I have no idea how she planned and carried out all of this. My agents are to contact me if there is anything that appears to be out of the ordinary.

"Is she staying at the hotel?" Danielle asked. "No, she isn't. The employee is staying in the suite. She has rented an expensive, furnished home outside of the city. She just recently sold her family home and put everything in storage, and it looks as though she has no plans to return.

"I have more news that you need to brace yourself for," Simms added. The employee is "Craig Carter," your ex-fiancé, Mrs. Carlisle.

"What!!?" Kim gasped. What, why, how does she even know him?" she asked, tears now filling her eyes. "We suspect Mrs. Harris paid to obtain as much information about you as she could and decided to use it to get to you. In the wake of my conversation with the gentleman, I don't think he has any idea or knows about her or anything about your life since your breakup," Simms speculated.

During our investigation, it also appears he needs whatever amount of money she is paying him. It must be a substantial amount because he has been seen spending large amounts in the city.

Mrs. Harris is also using her maiden name, "Wilder," when it suits her. "Wilder, Wilder?" Danielle said, starting to think. She was puzzled but remembered her encounter with someone with the same last name.

Wait a minute, there was an older woman who came into the gym weeks ago but never mentioned her first name, only her last name, "Wilder." She appeared to be interested in joining the gym, but I never heard back from her. I remember during our conversations, she mentioned that she had seen pictures of me at your wedding in a magazine, but then moved on to ask a question about Kim that I brushed off. I presume that after I didn't give her the information she wanted, I was no longer of use to her. She went through the motions of touring the facility as though she were interested and said she would contact us if she planned to join. That was it. She went to get on the treadmill, and I never saw her again.

"Do you think you would remember what she looked like, Ms. Moore?" Simms asked. "I—I believe so," she replied. "Is this the woman?" Simms asked, showing her a photo of Raven. Danielle looked at the photo, surprised, then closed her eyes and exhaled. "That's her," Danielle acknowledged. So, do you think she was probing me for information about Kim, as she pointed to herself? I don't know why I didn't catch on. "You would not have known about it," Simms conceded. Keep in mind, Ms. Moore, that she was using a name you weren't familiar with. She made sure of that before she got there.

"Wait a minute, I remember something else," Danielle recounted. When my employee asked her for her first name when setting up the appointment, she said Raven appeared agitated on the phone, so to eliminate an argument or complaint, she told her it was okay and that the last name would be fine. I didn't think to ask Mrs. Harris when speaking with her either.

Why didn't I pick up on that? How stupid could I be? she said, softly hitting her forehead. With tears in her eyes, Danielle looked over at Kim, whispering, "I am so sorry. I didn't know." Kim walked over to Danielle and gave her a hug to try and console her. "It's okay," Kim said. Looking at Simms, Kim asked, very upset at this point, "Is there a possibility that Mrs. Harris could be targeting Danielle too?" "I'm not so sure if she is or not, but given what Ms. Moore just said, there is a strong possibility.

Since the two of you were involved with Mr. Harris, I wanted to be sure to let all of you know what I discovered," Simms said. And another thing... Mr. Carlisle, I don't feel it's safe for your wife to stay here for a while. If my instincts are correct, it is only a matter of time before whatever Mrs. Harris has planned or whatever her motive is, she will probably be putting it into motion soon.

"Move out of my home?" Kim cried. "Do not move; just go somewhere you will be safe until we feel there is no longer a threat to you or your family. And in your condition, I am determined to keep you safe, Mrs. Carlisle," Simms said sternly. Kim noticed Xander's melancholy as she pivoted toward him. "If she has to leave, then I will too," Xander argued. "No, Mr. Carlisle, we need you here," Simms said firmly. Your housekeeper will be with her. We've already made arrangements for the two of them to stay in a hotel outside of the Chicago city limits, where they will be guarded by agents dressed in civilian clothing.

"What?" Kim said, crying uncontrollably. "It'll be okay," Simms sympathized. We hope it will only be for a little while. "Why do you need me?"

Xander asked, looking over at Simms. "We need you and Mrs. Moore to be a part of our sting operation," Simms commented. "Me?" Danielle asked. Why? "I've devised a plan, and hopefully, she will fall for it and take the bait," he said. "What is it?" Xander asked as he and Kim looked over at Danielle.

"Well, first of all, I need Mrs. Carlisle to show Danielle how to take the Zoom call for the commissioned art. Again, like I said, I don't believe Mr. Carter is aware of Raven's plans, and we want to make this as authentic and genuine as possible. Ms. Moore, do you think you can handle that?" Simms asked with concern. "For my best friend, you bet I can," she assured him. "Then I need you to pack a bag and get back here as soon as possible," he replied. One of my agents will accompany you to your place of residence. Also, Mrs. Carlisle, I need you and your housekeeper to do the same, and someone will take you to your destination.

People, we need to move quickly, and the sooner, the better. Mr. Carlisle, you can have your office schedule the appointment for tomorrow as early as possible. "Yes, sir, right away," Xander replied. Simms, is all of this really necessary? "Yes, Mr. Carlisle, it is," he replied. My intuition tells me that anyone who would go to such great lengths as Mrs. Harris has must be up to something, and I'm sure of it. Now, we need to get started. Everyone nodded and began doing what Investigator Simms insisted they do.

Chapter 39

Craig received a call later in the evening from Monica, Kim's administrator, to schedule an early morning appointment the following day. She gave him the Zoom link for the meeting to be conducted at 9:30 a.m. He was so excited that Designs, etc., had finally returned his call. "Mr. Carter, the designer will be online on time, so please be punctual," Monica explained. "Yes, ma'am, I will," Craig replied.

Raven had not come by to see him but instead emailed to check on him. After he read the email, Craig smiled at himself, thinking of how it was the best sex he ever had. Raven impressed him with her diverse poses and tender licks all over his body. Now, it was time for him to get back to his professional responsibilities. Feeling slightly shy, he didn't want to call, but he kept in the back of his mind that this was work and he was getting paid for it. Systematically, Craig did what he was instructed to do, so he picked up the business cell phone and dialed her number.

When her phone rang, Raven looked and saw the number, knowing immediately that it was Craig. "Hello, this is Ms. Harris," she said professionally. "Hi, Ms. Harris, this is Craig Carter," calling to confirm that I have spoken with Designs, etc., and our meeting is scheduled for 9:30 tomorrow morning. "Thank you, Craig. Are you clear on the dimensions, color scheme, and shapes of the required artwork?" Raven asked. "That's what I want to make sure of," he replied. I understand that it is two abstracts that are commissioned, correct? "Yes, good memory, Craig," she said. Please make sure to let the designer know that our customer wants it within the next week. "Yes, ma'am, I remember," he confirmed. "Do you have any other questions?" Raven asked. "No, I've got it," he replied.

Raven took a deep breath and said, "If there's nothing else, Craig immediately interjected. "Ms. Harris, Are you okay? I mean, about the other night. We haven't had an opportunity to talk about it." "Craig, I would rather not discuss this right now," she said. You have a job to do, Craig. When everything has been solidified regarding the artwork, let me know. Raven was now in her element and focused directly on her plan. "Yes, Ms. Harris," he replied, not to agitate her further, and hung up. Maybe she was embarrassed, he thought.

In the meantime, he changed from his suit to leisure wear since his workday was over. He then called Kate to check on her and their daughter before going to dinner. She was excited about the purchases he sent home and expressed how much they had missed him. He returned the sentiment, not forgetting the night he shared with Raven, knowing it was wrong of him.

Raven sat at home, relishing the thought of how her plan was falling into place and being close to the finish line. Her hatred and resentment had run deep for Kim. She told herself that all she wanted from her was a conversation about her son, but Kim rejected her demand. Raven became enraged and decided she would ensure Kim suffered the fate of losing a child and would not become the happy mother she planned to be.

With the illusion that it wasn't significant or didn't matter, Raven's thoughts shifted to the sexual encounter she had with Craig. "I could use another one of those nights," she said with a devious smile. Who knows? Maybe I will do just that again. With a couple of drinks, it would certainly take the edge off.

With a cunning smile, she stood up and went to the kitchen to prepare a broiled steak and a salad to enjoy with a bottle of wine. I ended up in bed with Craig due to excessive drinking, she laughed to herself. Only this time, she would be drinking her alcoholic beverages alone.

Craig returned to his hotel suite after dinner. He went to the mini bar, grabbed a couple of beers, and sat himself down on the plush sofa. He took a swig of one of the beers and leaned back, looking up at the gold crystal chandelier. His thoughts slowly drifted to the night with Raven and the excitement and arousal she instilled in him. "Why am I feeling this way? Why do I need her in my bed again?" he asked as he tried to take another sip of his beer. She had pleased him like no other woman could, including Kate.

Deep in his thoughts, Craig did everything to stay focused on his family. Despite not being married yet, plans were in the works upon his return home. For a brief moment, negative thoughts began to cross his mind. Why did I cheat on my family? But the answer faded away as his mind teetered back to Raven and their deeply intimate connection.

Constantly, Craig thought about how magical it felt to climax at the same time. He has never had that type of feeling, and he wanted more. It had been days since that night, and he wondered how Raven felt about what had occurred between the two of them. He attempted to discuss the issue with her, but she dismissed him as if the incident had never occurred. The more he thought about her the more his body dripped with sweat, and his private parts began to rise.

He finished the second beer, got up to take a lukewarm shower, and closed his eyes with thoughts of Raven as the water fell on his naked body. He wanted her but knew it was unlikely it would ever happen again. After showering, Craig retired for the night to ensure a good night's sleep for his meeting the following day.

Chapter 40

Craig was up early, organizing himself for the Zoom meeting with the designer. He had no idea who or whom he would see or speak to on the screen, so he wanted to be as professional as possible.

Raven is under the impression that Craig will be speaking with Kim, unknown that Danielle would be taking the call, believing Kim's guard would be down, and the two would reminisce about the good times they shared years ago as she took the order.

Craig turned on the computer and clicked the link for the meeting. The screen showed the message "waiting on the host," which didn't surprise him, given he was a little early.

Although Craig would only see her from the chest up on the screen, Danielle was also dressed professionally in a navy two-piece pantsuit with a white bow-neck blouse. She sat upright in the desk chair and opened the link, and Craig was already there. Kim ran several drills to ensure Danielle would be proficient. They exchanged pleasantries and introductions. Danielle, professionally mannered, asked the question, "So, Mr. Carter, I have noted here that you need two abstract artworks. Is that correct?" "Yes, Ms.?" Danielle stopped him, "You can call me Danni with an "I" instead of a "Y," she replied. "Yes, Danni and I have all the information regarding what's needed," he replied.

"Great, well, let's get started," Danielle commented. Craig described everything needed in detail, including the dimensions and coordinated colors. He also explained that the customer needs the artwork in the next 7 days. Would that be a problem?" he asked. "No, Mr. Carter, that won't be a problem at all," she said. And will you be picking up the artwork? "No, the owner is having a courier do the honors," Craig answered. But please contact me when the work is complete and ready. "We certainly will, Mr. Carter," Danielle said. Now, will there be anything else for you? "No, I believe that's everything," he replied.

"Okay, Mr. Carter, we will need a deposit for half of the cost today, and you can make the payment through our office by credit card. Please take down this order number and use it when you call the office to make your payment. I will be alerted to the transaction, and we will get started right away on your abstracts. Craig immediately pulled out his legal pad and pen and jotted down the information. "It has been a pleasure speaking with you, Mr. Carter. Design's etc. appreciates your order, and we look forward to working with you again in the near future," Danielle cordially replied. "Thank you, Danni, and I look forward to hearing from you soon," Craig said in response.

The meeting call took nearly an hour. After closing out the link, Craig picked up the business phone to call Raven. He confirmed that the meeting was a breeze and that everything went well. Raven wanted to ask him about Kim but held back. She was hesitant to engage in any actions or words that could potentially raise suspicion. So she continued to express positive words to Craig, knowing full well that things were about to change. Eventually, her fake business will close down, and when the time is right, she will come up with a justification to diminish Craig's position and move on with her agenda. Raven thanked him and they hung up. Suddenly, her mindset turned back to the night she shared with Craig and how he made her feel. She placed her phone on the table and subsequently dismissed her thoughts.

Later in the afternoon, Raven was feeling him again. "I wonder," she said to herself. Is it still too early to call Craig or wait a while, then make an impromptu call to congratulate him again on his excellent work performance? Then, out of the blue, she offers to treat him to dinner and drinks in his room. She would wear something more enticing than the professional suit she usually wore. Raven hopes that when he sees her appearance, he will change his facial expression quickly. She would then make advances toward him after dinner and a few drinks to see if the feeling was mutual and if he would be a willing participant.

Craig went out for the afternoon without changing clothes to tour more of the city since there was nothing more for him to do that day. Raven gave him permission for a rental car, but he preferred to take in the sites without driving. He walked in and out of stores on the West Loop, making purchases only for himself while admiring the unique architectural design of the buildings.

With packages in tow, he hailed a taxi to visit the Navy Pier. The taxi driver pointed out renowned landmarks and the overhead "L" trains as he drove the scenic route. When they reached the Navy Pier, Craig felt famished and tired. He stopped at a pizza parlor in the plaza of the Pier and had a large slice of pizza and a Coke while enjoying the view of patrons riding the 200-foot-high Ferris wheel.

After sitting for a considerable time, Craig returned to the Congress Plaza for the evening. By this time, it was right around 7 p.m. Craig grabbed a small bottle of wine from the mini bar and sat down on the sofa while loosening his tie and kicking off his shoes. He sat for a while, and then he began to contemplate his dinner plans.

As various thoughts crossed his mind, his cell phone rang. It was the business phone, so he knew it was Raven, but he wondered why she was calling this late, which he thought was out of character for her. "Hello, Ms. Harris, How are you?" he answered. "Hi, Craig, I wanted to congratulate you again for the tremendous job you did this morning and thought I would give you a call to see what you were doing this evening," she commented. Have you had dinner yet?" she inquired. "No, in fact, I was just thinking about that," he replied. "Then, I have a suggestion, why don't I come over, and we can order a nice dinner from room service and have a few drinks, then sit back and relax?" Raven urged. I know that you had a busy morning, and my day was full too. "Sure, of course, why not?" Craig replied. "Okay, well, I'll be there in about an hour," she said. Go ahead and order a bottle of champagne. "Sure, I'll do it right now," he happily replied.

When hanging up, Craig wondered about the change in Raven's attitude because, before now, she had avoided him and not been around. After their shared night, he was well aware that this was something she did not want to relive. She would only send one email every other day. Craig shrugged his shoulders, brushed off his thoughts, and said to himself, "I just can't figure women out," and called for room service.

In the meantime, Raven got ready for a night of fun, and hopefully, her sexual cravings for him would be satisfied. She sprayed on sensuous perfume and dressed in a partially sheered dress that revealed just enough to get Craig's attention. When she finished dressing, Raven viewed herself in the mirror and smiled. "This dress should do the trick," she said, tilting her head to one side. She put on a short jacket due to the coolness in the air and took an Uber to the hotel instead of driving.

When she arrived at the hotel, Raven took one last look at herself in the shiny gold-rimmed glass as the doorman opened the door for her. She walked in through the revolving doors into the hotel lobby. Her dress was above the knee, shimmering, and giving off a young, sexy, stylish appearance. She was feeling herself, looking as though she were the bell of the ball.

When Raven reached the hotel suite, she knocked on the door. Craig opened the door, and his jaw dropped. "You look great! Ms. Harris," he said. "Thank you, Craig... Now, can I come in?" she asked. Craig was in a daze, and that's exactly what Raven was hoping for. Hesitating and stumbling over his own words, Craig replied, "Yeah, sure, sure, please come in and make yourself comfortable. Craig watched her from behind and thought she appeared captivating.

I'll get the champagne and some glasses," he said. Blissfully, Raven strutted over to the sofa, sat down, and crossed her legs. Craig returned with the chilled champagne in an iced canister and two glasses, placing it all down on the mahogany gold-inlay coffee table. "Should I pour you a glass, Ms. Harris?" he asked. "Yes, please...and Craig, you can call me Elaina," she said. "Yes, ma'am, then quickly correct himself, Elaina," he replied.

"Would you like to order dinner now?" he asked, slightly nervous. "No, not yet. Let's have a glass or two of this delicious champagne before dinner," Raven alluringly said. "Sure, no problem," Craig replied. Craig carefully poured two glasses and handed one to Raven. She took a sip, then asked, sitting down her glass, "So, Craig, what did you do the rest of the day?" "Oh, I did some shopping for myself this time," he said. They both laughed. I walked the city streets, visited the Navy Pier, window-shopped, and purchased a few items from the Tatum Men's store in downtown Chicago.

"Oooo, I love the Pier at night," Raven lovingly said. The lights on the Ferris wheel are spectacular. My favorite time is to go during the holidays. Everyone's all wrapped up in the extremely cold, wintry weather, and the sound of carols is constantly blasting with the wind. Yes, sweetheart, the holidays are great here. "Wow, I need to bring my family to Chicago during that time," he said. "Yes, you must. They would certainly enjoy all of the holiday festivities, Raven commented.

After enjoying the entire bottle of champagne, Raven suggested they should probably have dinner before it got too late. Daily menus are provided for the hotel suites. Craig picked up the menu off the table, and Raven moved closer to review today's menu and place their order. "How about some oysters as an appetizer?" Raven suggested. Craig nodded and replied, "Yes, that sounds good." Craig ordered pasta Alfredo, and Raven ordered shrimp pasta and added another bottle of champagne. It took about thirty minutes before their meals arrived.

They sat at the dining table, engaging in random conversations and drinking more champagne. It seemed as though hours passed before the two of them were laughing uncontrollably and savoring the mood of a bonded friendship. They completed their meals and moved back to the sofa with the remaining champagne, laughing and touching each other as though they were best friends, but the feelings were much stronger than they ever knew.

After a few moments, the laughter turned into staring into each other's eyes as they moved closer to each other. Craig felt the heat between them, but out of fear of rejection, he froze in a childish state of panic. Raven could see what was happening, so she kicked off her heels and put one leg across his, asking him to rub her feet and massage her leg due to the pain from the shoes.

Craig sensed she was making seductive advances. He began slowly massaging her foot and stimulating the blood flow in each of her toes. Raven held her head back, making moaning and groaning sounds. She then raised her head, looking at him, and began licking her lips until they were juicy and wet.

Craig was so mesmerized that he could see the light reflecting off her lips as her tongue went back and forth in a sucking motion. She took her hand and moved the hair on the right side of her face to the back of her ear, exposing her earring, then slid her hand down the side of her face. "It's a little warm in here, don't you think, Craig?" she questioned.

"Maybe, a little, I'll check the thermostat," he said as he gently removed her leg to get up from the sofa. He returned after adjusting the temperature and sat down, gently placing her legs on his lap to continue massaging her foot. "That feels so good," she said. Craig smiled in delight. He then moved his hand upward to her leg and eventually to her thigh. Raven relaxed her legs, moaning with glee as his hands moved up and down her legs.

After slowly moving his hands further, he realized she was not wearing any underwear, so he moved his hands toward her vaginal area. She did not stop him, but instead slid down so he could get closer to the area. Once he felt he had arrived at the spot, he slowly began rubbing the inside of her, and she moaned much more. Raven then slid down further to get more comfortable.

She pulled up the sheer part of her dress that exposed her entire vaginal area. Craig was now so excited that he could not stop himself.

And Raven was glad to let him have his way with her. She rose after a few minutes, removed her dress and bra, dropped them to the floor, and walked toward the bedroom. She turned to look at Craig provocatively before entering the room. He appeared to be in shock, but then snapped out of it and got up to follow her.

As he got closer, she pulled him lightly into the room. Craig removed his clothing as he walked to the bed where Raven had laid herself down in splendor. He took her by the hand and helped her up from the bed to pull back the comforter, then slowly picked her up and gently placed her under the covers. He then joined her. As their bodies slowly intertwined, the rhythm of their moans of ecstasy echoed in unison.

Raven got what she had come for, and momentarily, it satisfied her mind, body, and soul.

Chapter 41

Xander and Investigator Simms praised Danielle for her professionalism in taking the fake artwork order. "Now, we have only a few days to put the remaining plan in order," Simms commented. I have replaced Kim's identity with one of our female officers, who will arrive in a few minutes. I need the cars of both Ms. Moore and Mrs. Carlisle locked in the garage on the day of the pickup. I didn't notice, but are there small window inserts in your garage doors, Mr. Carlisle? "No, sir, there isn't," Xander replied. "Good, then we will need your vehicle parked in the driveway," Simms said. We need the outside of your home to appear as normal as possible. When the replacement officer arrives here, we will go through the steps to make this plan as tight as possible.

In the meantime, Mr. Carlisle, would you get the artwork Mrs. Carlisle described so it will be available to see once Ms. Harris enters the door? "Yes, sir," Xander replied as he left the room. "Ms. Moore, you will be in the room of the housekeeper that's located off from the kitchen area. You will be equipped with an earpiece to listen in on the conversations going on in the house," Simms explained.

As he talked, the female officer, who would be impersonating Kim Carlisle, arrived. Simms opened the door to let Officer Janet Waldrop in. He made the introductions to Xander and Danielle and explained her role. In shock, they silently stared at the officer, who bore a close resemblance to Kim. "Are you pregnant?" Danielle asked. "Oh, no, ma'am. I'm wearing a silicone pregnancy belly," Officer Janet replied. We located one just the right size for the number of months of Mrs. Carlisle's pregnancy. I'm just trying to get used to wearing it. "Waldrop, Simms interrupted. "Mr. Carlisle will show you to your room, where you can get comfortable." "Yes, yes, well, come this way." Xander motioned to the officer as he turned to look over his shoulder. He was still surprised at how closely her appearance resembled Kim. The officer followed him up the stairs to a bedroom closest to the entrance hallway. "This is so beautiful, and the artwork design visually draws your eyes all around the room," Officer Waldrop said with amazement. "Thanks to my wife," Xander asserted as he left the room.

When the officer returned to the makeshift headquarters room, Simms pulled everyone together and explained the logistics of the plan he had put in place. Xander and Danielle looked at each other, surprised at how carefully detailed he was.

"I can't believe this is happening to us," Xander sighed with his head bowed. When will it all end with this crazy-ass family?" he asked as he raised his head. "Mr. Carlisle, if I didn't think Ms. Harris was up to something, I wouldn't put you and your family through all of this," Simms said, trying to ease Xander's nervousness about the situation. I truly believe that my instincts are on the money, especially after Ms. Moore informed us of Harris visiting her establishment and attempting to get information about your wife. That is just one of the incidents that confirmed my thoughts about Harris, and that became a little too unsettling, which is why I continued to look further into her life.

Everything I primarily found out in my investigation let me know that something was off with her, and I decided not to take any chances this time around. What happened to her son has her beyond grief and out for revenge; otherwise, why would she go to such great lengths by coming to Chicago to set up a fake business and employ your wife's ex-fiancé?

You wouldn't expect any ordinary grieving mother to uproot her life and move to another state away from her immediate family and friends. I'm 99% sure that I'm right, Mr. Carlisle, so please, just be patient with me, sir. I promise you, this will all be over soon. Xander reluctantly nodded, replying, "Okay, I understand, and thank you for looking out for me and my family. Would it be okay if I called my wife?" he asked. "Yeah, go ahead. Please do not expose anything that we've talked about here," Simms instructed. I need your wife to stay calm. "Yes, sir. Sure," Xander replied.

Xander called Kim to let her know everything was fine and that he was not in danger. To raise her spirits, he told her to say hello to the baby for him, and they would be coming home soon. They both laughed when she said that Dada said hello as she rubbed her stomach. After talking with Kim, he asked to speak with Isabel.

When speaking with Isabel, he stressed the importance of keeping Kim calm and composed since she is about two weeks away from giving birth to little Carlisle. Isabel assured him she was being well taken care of, and there was no need to worry. After saying their goodbyes, Xander retired to his room for the evening. He felt at ease knowing that Kim and Isabel were safe and that everything was going as planned.

Four days had gone by, and it was now time to move on to Phase II of Simms's plan. Danielle was instructed to send pictures via email of the abstracts to Craig Carter for approval and to schedule the pickup. Sitting at his desk, Craig heard the email notification sound and opened the mail to find pictures of the artwork. He immediately called Raven, and she requested that he send them to her as soon as possible.

After she received them, she called Craig back and requested a date and time for pickup. Craig called the office and spoke with Monica, who confirmed the remaining balance. He paid the balance, and then Monica put him on hold while she called Xander. Xander informed Simms that the pickup was being scheduled. Simms, in turn, requested that Monica schedule it for the following day. That would give him and the others enough time to go over everything again. Xander relayed the instructions, and Monica returned to the phone and scheduled pickup for 11 a.m. the following day.

Craig called Raven and gave her the information. Briefly, she recalled her actions to seek revenge on Eric's adversary. Her smile transformed from one of inner struggle to one of triumph. Unknowingly, Craig not only fed her body and soul with a steady diet, but in the process, he overfed her ego. She was amazed by the rapid pace at which everything was falling into place. Raven thanked Craig and requested he meet her for lunch at Nando's in downtown Chicago. Craig was thrilled to get the invite and promptly replied with a yes.

When Craig arrived for lunch, Raven was already sitting at a table in a corner of the restaurant. "Have a seat, Craig," she said. How has your day gone so far? "Very well, thank you," Craig answered, appearing puzzled. "I've got some good news for you," Raven said, smiling. Since you've done such a good job, I'm giving you some time off. You can go home and spend time with your family and friends. I'll contact you when I want you to return, probably in the next two to three weeks. How does that sound? "That's great! Thank you, Ms. Harris," Craig excitedly replied. "Also, I trust you, Craig, so I'm going to give you the remainder of your pay, and I will make sure the expenses for you to return will be taken care of," she said, giving him a huge smile and an envelope with the money.

So, after lunch, you can return to the hotel and pack. Leave everything else in the room, and I'll pick it up later. An Uber will be waiting for you at 6:30 a.m. tomorrow to take you to the Amtrak station for the 8 a.m. train. So, go ahead and contact your family to let them know you're coming home. "You don't know how much this means to me," Craig said. Thank you so much! "You're very welcome, and thank you for a job well done," Raven replied. Craig knew that she was thanking him for more than just the job, and he smiled back at her.

Chapter 42

Raven returned to the home she was renting and started to pack. Once she accomplished her mission, she would leave Chicago immediately. One thing she forgot to do was contact Kim's office to make sure that her husband would be there at the office when she went to pick up the artwork.

She was unaware that Investigator Simms's ultimate plan was to have Xander move his vehicle to the garage and place Kim's car in the driveway. Simms also made arrangements with the security company of the subdivision to allow one of his officers to handle that day's assignment of gate duties.

Raven called the office and spoke with receptionist Cathy, who put her through to Monica. "Yes, this is Monica; how can I help you?" she said. "Yes, my name is Ms. Wilder, and I am due to pick up an artwork piece tomorrow morning. I wanted to know if Mr. Carlisle would be present when I arrived. I wanted to meet him as well. "I'm afraid not, Ms. Wilder. Mr. Carlisle will be in the office if you would like to come by," Monica replied. "Sure, that will be great," Raven said, holding back her excitement. "Oh, and Ms. Wilder, please call the designer Kim Carlisle on her cell phone the morning of pickup to let her know when you're on your way," Monica reminded her. "I certainly will, Monica; thank you," Raven replied. Please tell Mr. Carlisle I will come by after picking up my portraits, if that's okay. "I'm sure that will be fine, Ms. Wilder. I will let him know. "Thank you, Monica. Have a good evening," Raven said and hung up.

Monica immediately contacted Xander about the phone call. To make the talk audible to Investigator Simms, Xander turned up the volume. "Thank you, Monica, for letting me know. Take care," he said. As he hung up, Xander turned to Simms and commented, "You were right again, as usual." "Just staying a step ahead, sir," Simms commented. Now the stage is set.

Raven continued packing and placing items in her car. She wasn't that hungry for dinner but instead opened up a bottle of wine, sat down on the sofa, and started visualizing her strategy of keeping Kim off guard. "Tomorrow would be the day," she said to herself. My son would then be able to rest in peace, and that bitch would be grieving. Raven then began thinking of Kim's friend, Danielle, and going after her next, but everything she had put in place had become too exhausting. "Maybe another time," she thought. After creating a fake business and spending an enormous amount of money, it would all be worth it. She felt now, after everything, that a real vacation would be on the horizon.

The officers following Raven routinely updated her location, so Simms knew she was at the rental house. After finishing up their takeout meals, Xander, Danielle, Janet, and Simms sat quietly at the table. "Hopefully, this will all be over tomorrow," Simms said, trying to spread some positivity to break the silence. Officer Waldrop chimed in, "Yeah, we got this."

Looking exhausted, Xander and Danielle looked up from their takeout plates with a half-smile. They were deeply absorbed in their personal issues, leading to a recollection of the past. "We know," Xander replied. I just want all of this to be over and my family to be back home. "So do we," Simms said. After putting their plates in the trash can, everyone retired to their designated area for the evening, and Simms returned to the command center to go over their plans for tomorrow.

The next morning, Raven woke up early, feeling groggy from the wine the night before. She got up, took a shower, and dressed comfortably in a navy two-piece suit with low heels. Then she made a pot of coffee, boiled two eggs, and buttered her toast. Raven ate her breakfast in silence, thinking of her son Eric as she reflected on the circumstances. "It ends today, Son. You will now have the respect you deserve. I know you didn't want to hurt yourself, and I know some circumstances made it hard for you. Momma has always been there and always will be."

Raven continued to sit, drinking her second cup of coffee, with tears in her eyes. The worst thing that could have happened to her was losing Eric. Regretfully, she will always have a great void in her heart. She believed that what she was doing was the right thing, not necessarily for herself but for her only child. Raven is determined to alleviate her pain, even if it means causing harm to Kim and her unborn child. She wiped tears from her eyes and realized she needed to remain strong for her son.

Eagerly, she got up from the table to look at the time. It was 9:30 a.m. She took a deep breath and exhaled a huge sigh of relief. Almost "showtime," she thought. Raven walked into the living room, sat on the sofa, put her head in her hands, and prayed.

Thank you, Lord, for helping me get this far. They say you don't make any mistakes, but you have made plenty in my life. Now, you have taken the most important person in my life, Eric. This time, I'm not asking for any help. Just make sure my son is watching over me as I take care of the people who mistreated him. Amen.

Removing her hands and looking straight up to heaven, she said, "Real Justice Will Now Be Served."

Chapter 43

Craig left the hotel happy as a lark. After he turned in the key to his suite, Craig was informed that the room charges had been paid. He nodded and headed to the front doors to see his Uber on time, as Raven confirmed. When arriving at the Amtrak station, he attempted to tip the driver but was told it had already been paid. Craig and the driver exited the car, and the driver unloaded his bags. Fortunately, he sent his heavier items the day before, which was a logical decision.

Happily, Craig entered the station at the ticket desk, and again, as Raven stated, his boarding ticket was awaiting his arrival. Craig then took a seat and opened a magazine that he had brought with him. He saw an ad for a consulting company, and his mind began to wonder about the job and Ms. Harris. He couldn't understand his feelings for her. Craig questioned himself about whether it was lustful sex or love for her and the bonus of sex. He was left with many questions about himself. Suddenly, his mind was jolted back to reality when he heard his train number.

After sitting for another hour, Raven got up to leave for Kim's residence. Everything was ready and in place. She locked the house door, placed the key in one of the flower pots near the front door, and got in her car. She notified the owner earlier of an emergency in her family and said she would be leaving but would pay out the lease. The landlord and his wife felt bad for Raven's situation and advised her to pay only three months of the remaining lease. Raven smirked and advised him that she would forward the money right away. She sent the money via the Cash App in three transactions. The landlord confirmed receipt, and Raven put on her seatbelt and drove off.

In the meantime, Simms went over everything once more. Officer Waldrop's wire was checked for covert listening, and Danielle's earpiece was tested for sound accuracy. Simms indicated that he and additional officers would be nearby, listening to their conversations. If nothing became of anything other than Ms. Harris picking up the artwork, they would move in right away.

"Are you sure this is going to work?" Xander inquired. "Mr. Carlisle, as I said before, as Simms looked him straight in the eyes, I want this to be over as much as you do." Just make sure you leave the room once you take Ms. Harris to the media room. "I will," Xander replied. Now, if there is nothing further, let's do this. Simms then left the house. Officer Waldrop, Xander, and Danielle walked to the media room where the artwork was sitting and took a seat. Things were tense, but they all knew what had to be done.

After about twenty minutes of sitting quietly, the officer posing as a guard called Simms to alert him that Ms. Harris had entered the subdivision. Simms called and informed Waldrop. Suddenly, the doorbell rang. Xander jumped up. Danielle quickly got up and quietly walked to Isabel's room. He viewed the outside camera, while Ms. Harris stood there, observing if anyone was watching her. Xander took one last deep breath and opened the door. "Ms. Wilder?" he asked. "Yes," Raven replied. "Come in, please," he said, leaning against the door. My wife is in the media room. Please come this way. Raven followed him down the hallway, admiring all of the décor and artwork along the way. "You have a nice home here, and the artwork is beautiful," she commented. "Thank you," Xander replied. But give all the credit to my wife. She is an excellent designer. "Yes, sir. That's the reason why I chose her studio to do the work," Raven declared.

As they reached the media room, Waldrop got up to greet her, and Xander left the room as instructed. "Hi, Ms. Wilder, extending her hand. I'm Kimberly Carlisle, but you can call me Kim," she said in a mild, meek tone. "Nice to finally meet you," Raven replied. Would you like something to drink while you're looking over the pieces?" Waldrop asked. "No, I've got a flight to catch, so I'll be brief," Raven replied. Smiling, Waldrop continued. Please excuse my wobbling, but as you can see, we're about to have our first little one. He or she is due in a week or so, and you are my last client before the arrival. Happily pointing to the artwork, Waldrop said, "Here are the pieces you ordered. I hope they're to your satisfaction." Raven walked over to the artwork, looked at the two pieces, turned, and calmly said, "Yes, yes, these are nice, very nice, but what I find the most intriguing, Ms. Carlisle, is you," she said, pulling out a gun from her jacket pocket.

"What, what are you doing?" Waldrop asked, appearing scared and panicky. "WHAT AM I DOING?" Raven viciously said as Xander peeked in, wanting to act, but all he could do was stay back so as not to interrupt the plan. "Bitch, I'm Mrs. Harris, Thomas Eric Harris' mother," she blurted out. She pointed the gun directly at Waldrop and said, I tried talking to you weeks ago about my son, and you, you winch, hung up on me. That wasn't the right thing to do. You see what I had to go through, bitch? I found other ways that cost me a fortune, so here I am. Let's talk! Simms had heard enough and directed his officers to move in.

Waldrop tried to slowly pull out her gun as Raven continued to rant but had trouble getting to it because of the silicone belly. Xander wondered what was happening and couldn't take it any longer. He walked into the room, and Raven quickly turned to him, yelling for him to sit down. Waldrop was still trying to get out her gun but could not reach it.

Danielle listened to the commotion, quietly opened the door to Isabel's room, and tipped out. Raven was waving the gun and making threats. "You took my son's affection for you and stepped on it! You didn't even bother to send a card or attend the funeral. Have you no heart, or are you simply passively defying the reputation of his good name? I know what he did, but you provoked it," Raven continued. My son would not have done anything to you or anybody else unless he was pushed or agitated. I blame you for that! I promised him while he lay in that casket that I would get justice for him, and today I am going to do just that. You took my son away from me, and now I'm going to return the favor as tears roll down her face.

By that time, Danielle could see the entire room, and Raven had a gun with her back turned away from her. "Put it down!" Danielle yelled. Raven turned and shot off one bullet. It struck Danielle in the left shoulder. Danielle then raised her right hand and shot Raven in the chest. Raven looked surprised and fell back, falling to the floor and dropping the gun.

Simms and his men kicked in the door, and everyone was hollering and screaming. Danielle was still holding her gun with a gunshot wound in her arm. Feeling devastated, Waldrop, in shock, rushed to her side. She took off her bolero and pressed it against the wound to stop the bleeding. Cautiously, Xander walked over to Raven, where she mumbled her son's name over and over again.

As Simms entered the room, he saw the result of what had happened and screamed for someone to call an ambulance. He grabbed the blanket from the sofa arm and pressed it on the wound in Raven's chest. "Hold on, hold on, Ms.

Harris," he encouraged. Raven's eyes were blinking slowly, and she never uttered another word.

Then Simms looked up at Danielle. "She was going to kill all of us," she said to Simms with a blank expression. I couldn't let her do that. Simms nodded to one of his officers to take the gun away from Danielle, while Xander ran to get something to stop the bleeding in her left arm. Danielle then closed her eyes, and she began to fall to the floor, possibly from shock. Officer Waldrop and another officer caught her, helping her to an armchair. Xander rushed over to her side with a thick towel to stop the bleeding. Slumped in the chair, Danielle took shallow breaths, closed and reopened her eyes, and looked at him, whispering, "It's over, it's over, Xander," and she began to cry in his arms.

The ambulance arrived, and EMTs checked Raven's vitals. One of them put her on an oxygen mask, while the other hooked her up to an IV. They then quickly put her on a gurney and wheeled her out to the ambulance. Simms looked at Danielle's wound, and it appeared the bullet had passed through the back of her arm without touching any vital organs. He and Waldrop put her in his police car. He turned on the blue lights and rushed her to the ER.

While en route, Simms called the detectives to gather evidentiary information of value and to make sure both guns were bagged and tagged.

Waldrop entered her police car with Xander, and they followed closely behind Simms. The remaining officers were instructed to secure the boundaries by surrounding the area with crime scene tape and to stay on guard until the investigating team finished their work. Also, do not give any information to the media; our spokesperson will release information as soon as possible.

Subsequently, the media heard about the incident before officers finished securing the scene. Some of them rushed to the Carlisle address, and others went to the Chicago Hospital ER. At the scene, yellow tape was being streamed as cameras flashed from all directions. Nearby neighbors stood at their doors, peeking out their windows, or wandered up and down their driveways, trying to see what happened. As the media walked through the neighborhood, most of the people refused to answer questions or covered their faces as the media approached them.

In the meantime, Raven's brother, Harold, was enjoying some time with his daughter, Kathy. Earlier, they went shopping for his grandchildren, and of course, his daughter threw a thing or two in the basket for herself. They laughed, talked, and reminisced about her childhood, and then bought a pizza for movie time. They sat down in the den with their coke, popcorn, and pizza to enjoy a movie they had heard so much about.

Within 30 minutes of the movie, there was a news break.

"We have breaking news that the mother of accused attempted murderer and rapist Thomas Eric Harris, identified as Raven Elaina Wilder Harris, was shot earlier this evening at the home of one of her son's victims, Kimberly Casey Carlisle. If you remember, three years ago, Eric Harris attacked Kimberly Casey and left her for dead in her prestigious downtown interior design studio. Details are sketchy right now as to why Ms. Harris was at the home. We have a crew on the scene and at the Chicago Hospital ER. Once we learn more, we will bring it to you tonight on the 11 o'clock newscast."

Harold and his daughter, Kathy, sat in total shock as tears rolled down their faces. "I knew something wasn't right, Dad," his daughter said. We should have forced Aunt Raven to get some help. "I tried several times, sweetheart, but she wouldn't do it," Harold said sadly. I didn't want to push her, so I left it alone. Now, I regret that I didn't try harder.

"Well, we've got to call the hospital and see what's going on," Kathy said. "Yeah, yeah, I know," Harold replied. He was confused and scared about the situation and did not feel positive about the outcome. Kathy called the Chicago Hospital but was given very little information about Raven. They sat there, hugging and crying, before both of their cell phones started ringing non-stop.

When the ambulance reached the hospital, the EMTs hurried to get out, opened the back doors, pulled the gurney while pressing the handle to release the wheel, and rushed Raven into the ER. The doctors were near the doors, waiting for their arrival. One EMT updated one of them on her vitals, while the others rushed Raven into the ER. Simms followed them but stopped at the doorway.

The doctors worked vigorously and rigorously to save her life. While standing at the door, Simms overheard two doctors discussing major damage to one of the vital organs and the fact that she had lost a lot of blood. One of them said, "After the blood transfusion, if she's stable, we've got to see if we can repair it." "We need blood right away," the other doctor said. Then he turned and asked the nurse to call the blood bank to get blood for patient number 0154. They prepared the patient by following the protocol for a blood transfusion.

When the blood arrived, one nurse put a blue band around Raven's wrist, indicating a blood transfusion in progress. Another nurse attached the saline solution and blood bag to the IV pole and observed Raven as fluid began to drip. She sat there another 30 minutes to make sure there was no blood product reaction. After working on Raven for four hours, the doctors looked at one another in silence. Finally, one of them said, "It's now up to her."

Chapter 44

Officer Simms went to the hospital cafeteria to get a bite to eat. He looked over the selection of dishes behind the food shield guard counter. "How can I help you?" the server asked. Simms pointed to the broccoli casserole and baked chicken, and she placed them on his plate. As he moved down the line, he stopped, filled his glass with sweet tea, and proceeded to the check-out counter. Steadily walking and balancing his tray, Simms sits next to a large window in the back of the dining hall. While looking out the window, he began to reminisce about what could have been done differently.

Being an officer for over 20 years, Simms knew that organizing and planning were the crust of a sting operation. He also knew that things could change in the blink of an eye, and you have to be alert to this possibility. Even though Danielle derailed the plan, she saved many lives from the wrath of Raven. Closing his eyes for a second, Officer Simms leaned back in his chair and muttered, "I can't forget the main part of the sting operation was to keep the Carlisle family and their unborn baby safe, which we did."

After finishing his meal, his mind went back to Raven Harris. He got up, put his plate in the caster, and returned to the ER. When he got there, the curtain around her bed was closed, so he sat on the leather loveseat in the hallway. Occasionally, he would glance up at her room, waiting patiently for an updated status report from the doctors. With trepidation, Simms got up from the sofa and began pacing the floor.

Minutes later, Simms peered into the door and asked, "Is she conscious?" "Barely," one doctor replied. "Do you mind if I try and talk to her?" he asked. "Sure, but for only a few minutes. She may not be able to respond to you," the doctor commented. "Thank you," Simms said. He walked closer to her, leaned, and whispered, "Ms. Harris, can you hear me?" Raven did not respond. He whispered two more times, until suddenly she slowly opened her eyes, barely turning her head toward him.

"Do you know what happened to you?" he asked. Blink if you can hear me. Raven blinks once. She then turned her head away from him. "Are you aware you're in the hospital?" he questioned. Raven slowly turned back to him and whispered, "I was doing it for my son. He needed to rest. Lord, have mercy on me, and she exhaled."

Just as she did, the heart machine she was hooked up to began to beep loudly, flashing various colors, and the digital numbers began to drop. Doctors rushed in and saw that her heart had stopped. Trying hard to revive her with the defibrillator paddles several times, they had to call it. Raven Elaina Wilder Harris was pronounced dead at 3:45 p.m.

The news of Raven's death was just released. Some crime shows have already demeaned Raven and her son, and others sympathize with Raven and belittle her son even though the whole story hasn't been told. Finally, Channel 44Promote reports live at the scene and the hospital.

Sergeant Scott stepped to the podium and explained the sting operation and what went right and what went wrong. He also talked about the goal of the operation, which was a success. The camera switched to the hospital. The hospital spokesperson stated that two people were injured, and one had succumbed to her injury. She is identified as Raven Elaina Wilder Harris, and she is from Detroit, Michigan. More news at 11 o'clock.

Again, Harold's daughter, Kathy, called the Chicago hospital. This time, she was able to speak to a hospital administrator. The worst they feared was now confirmed. Kathy lowered her head in tears, dropping the phone. Harold looked at her and knew his sister, Raven, was gone.

Craig got home and walked into his apartment, where Kate was waiting for him. Focused on the news, she didn't hear his footsteps as he entered the room. Being comical, he yelled, "Honey, I'm home. She didn't respond. Kate, what's wrong?" he asked. "Remember that guy I told you about a few years ago who tried to kill his ex-girlfriend?" she asked. "Yeah, what about him?" Craig asked nonchalantly. "His mother got shot at the ex-girlfriend's home earlier today, and they just announced that she died," Kate replied. "Really?" Craig said as he put his bags down. "Yeah, her name was Raven Harris," she commented. Craig turned quickly to Kate. "What did you say?" "Her name was Raven Harris, Thomas Eric Harris' mother. "Who was the ex-girlfriend?" he curiously asked. "I think her name was Kimberly... Kimberly Casey. She's been married for about a year to her CFO husband, Xander Carlisle," Kate said. Craig started to feel lightheaded. He couldn't believe that the woman, who was his boss, was the mother of an attempted murderer and a rapist. He then started to piece things together about why she hired him. It was because of his ex-fiancé. He now felt sick to his stomach. "Are you okay?" Kate asked him. "Yeah, sure," Craig replied.

My GOD! She was the woman who hired me to work for her. Did you know about what she was going to do?' Kate shouted. "No, of course not. Sure, I wondered certain things while I was there, but I figured it was her company, and she was paying me for a job to contact designers for artwork, so I just dismissed the thoughts, and that's it!

He then calmly said, "Now I know why she paid me all the money she promised and hurried to get me out of town." Anyway, it's not my problem now. Kate dramatically added, "I had a feeling something was up with her—the way she hurried you off to Chicago. "Are you sure you were not involved in that mess?" Kate asked. "I'm positive," Craig responded.

Craig then thought back to Investigator Simms. If he had thought I had anything to do with what Ms. Harris was planning, I know he would have done something right then, he said to himself. Craig didn't let on to the fact that he knew he had dodged a bullet. He had money now, and there was no reason that Kate would ever need to know what happened between him and Raven while he was in Chicago for anything other than work.

Epilogue

Raven Elaina Wilder Harris became a troubled soul after the death of her beloved son, Thomas Eric Harris. With the grief she endured, Raven turned to the attribution of blame and revenge. She decided that her life's work would be spent avenging those she thought were her son's adversaries, regardless of the task or the cost.

Danielle's injuries were treated and deemed non-life threatening. She was treated in the ER, and her left arm was placed in a sling for the next six to eight weeks. Kim and Xander were so appreciative of the quick reaction Danielle possessed in a time of crisis. Danielle and Kim hugged and cried as Danielle reaffirmed her promise of always being there for her.

Kim and her housekeeper, Isabel, returned home after the investigation was complete. A week later, Kim went into labor and delivered a beautiful, healthy baby girl. After a tender argument over a name for her, she and Xander decided on Tatiana Patrice. The arrival of Tatiana Patrice Carlisle filled their home with happiness, and the threat posed by Raven gradually faded into the background.

In addition to being kept on as the housekeeper, Isabel received much-needed time off to be with her family. They celebrated her with traditional dinners and enjoyable games Despite their questions about the incident, Isabel didn't discuss anything beyond what was featured and heard on the news, fearing they would discourage her from returning to the Carlisle family.

When Isabel returned to the Carlisle's home, she felt the love and happiness radiating from the proud parents as she watched them gaze in awe at little Tatiana. The threat of Raven Harris was finally over, allowing them to breathe a little easier.

Even though Simms didn't like the fact that Danielle brought a gun to the scene, he testified that they found themselves in imminent danger and had no other choice but to defend themselves. Mrs. Harris, despite being warned to put the gun down, shot Ms. Moore in the arm and she returned fire striking Mrs. Harris in the chest.

Simms was upset that Danielle brought a gun, which was not in his plans, but she had the right to protect herself and others as a licensed firearms owner.

Although the outcome was tragic, Simms expressed gratitude for trusting his instincts while feeling sorrow and grief for the Harris family.

Danielle testified that after her terrifying experience years earlier, she was left vulnerable and decided she would be trained and licensed to carry a firearm. The way Raven was waving around the gun between Officer Waldrop and Xander Carlisle, she knew she had to do something. With tears in her eyes, Danielle stated that she was not proud of shooting Mrs. Harris, but she was glad she saved their lives. Danielle was exonerated of any charges and found to have acted in self-defense.

As for Craig Carter, he is enjoying the fruits of his labor with Kate and their daughter. Craig finally finished college and has a permanent job, and there have been no further conversations about his time in Chicago. The year after receiving a lucrative position, Craig and Kate got married and are looking forward to their future.

About a month after Raven's burial, her will and testament was read to the family by her estate attorney. Most of her fortune was left to her brother, Harold, with a note suggesting he travel the world. She also left money for Kathy and her children. The children's money will be kept in trust for their education or until they reach the age of 30.

As Harold reviewed his copy of the will, he was in complete shock at how much money he and Kathy inherited and wondered where Raven had gotten all that money. Without a doubt, he was well aware that Raven had probably taken all of those secrets to her grave. Her troubled life was effectively disguised in a fairytale of lies, impacting not only herself but also her loving family. Despite the deep emotional impact of the tragedy, they cultivated a deep understanding of each other's emotions during this challenging time.